AF484877

RECEIVING AND MAINTAINING GOD'S REVIVAL IN YOUR LIFE AND IN THE LOCAL CHURCH

Volume 3

DOING WHAT CAN BRING DOWN GOD'S REVIVAL

STEPHEN ADU-BOAHEN

Receiving and Maintaining God's Revival in your Life and in the Local Church Copyright © 2024 by Stephen Adu Boahen. All Rights Reserved.

All rights reserved. No part of this book may be reproduced in any form or by any electronic or mechanical means including information storage and retrieval systems, without permission in writing from the author. The only exception is by a reviewer, who may quote short excerpts in a review.

Scriptures marked NIV are taken from the NEW INTERNATIONAL VERSION (NIV): Scripture taken from THE HOLY BIBLE, NEW INTERNATIONAL VERSION ®. Copyright© 1973, 1978, 1984, 2011 by Biblica, Inc.™. Used by permission of Zondervan

Scriptures marked NKJV are taken from the NEW KING JAMES VERSION (NKJV): Scripture taken from the NEW KING JAMES VERSION®. Copyright© 1982 by Thomas Nelson, Inc. Used by permission. All rights reserved.

Scriptures marked NLT are taken from the HOLY BIBLE, NEW LIVING TRANSLATION (NLT): Scriptures taken from the HOLY BIBLE, NEW LIVING TRANSLATION, Copyright© 1996, 2004, 2007 by Tyndale House Foundation. Used by permission of Tyndale House Publishers, Inc., Carol Stream, Illinois 60188. All rights reserved. Used by permission.

Scriptures marked GNB are taken from the GOOD NEWS BIBLE (GNB): Scriptures taken from the Good News Bible © 1994 published by the Bible Societies/HarperCollins Publishers Ltd UK, Good News Bible© American Bible Society 1966, 1971, 1976, 1992. Used with permission.

.
STEPHEN ADU BOAHEN
Visit my website at www.amazon.com/author/stephenadu-boahen

Table of Contents

INTRODUCTION

Knowing how to prepare some of the best foods and dishes in the world and actually applying this knowledge to be able to prepare some of the most sumptuous dishes are not the same. One is theoretical and one is practical. The availability of revivals in the church of Christ and our actually taking the right steps to be able to receive and maintain these revivals in the life of the local church are not the same.

You can learn and know all the important principles concerning profitable business and wealth creation theoretically and still remain one of the poorest people in your community, in your country and in the world! Knowing all the important truths and teachings about God's revivals alone without any practical application will never and can never bring you any practical revivals. This is the major focus and main highlight of this third volume in the series of four books on God's revival. It aims at showing us in specific terms some of the important and unavoidable steps we must take to be able to receive God's revivals regularly.

It goes further to show us in practical terms where to start, how to continue and where to finish if we truly desire God's genuine revivals at the personal level and generally in the life of the church. This explains why in various portions it is practical and balanced to the point of even proposing subjects and topics to deal with, the type of revival prayers to offer to God and how to organize major revival programmes effectively. This book can therefore be categorized as the book of practical action on the journey towards God's mighty spiritual revivals and spiritual awakenings. Read on to be able to apply the knowledge you have about how to receive God's revivals in practical terms!

CHAPTER ONE
THE CONDITIONS OF GOD'S REVIVAL (PART 1)

INTRODUCTION

Botanists tell us that seeds germinate only after the three conditions necessary for germination are met. These are the provision of air in the form of oxygen, the provision of water, and the provision of warmth in the form of the required temperature. Seeds can remain wherever they are for a long time without germinating unless these important conditions mentioned above are met conjunctly. In addition to these general conditions, we are further told that some seeds also require light to germinate while others require darkness to germinate. These are the conditions which must by every means be met before any seed germination can take place.

Revivals are just like these seeds because unless the required practical conditions are provided in the church and in our personal lives, they can never occur. In other words, any revivals engendered by the Holy Spirit just don't occur without our meeting some important practical conditions. This is to emphasize that when we create the right atmosphere for them and further provide the practical conditions for their outbreak, God will always pour down His revivals to bring us the desired spiritual renewals and spiritual restorations. This is the major content of this chapter which we want to examine. In short, we want to list and discuss some of these important and inevitable conditions and requirements to help us anytime we want to pray for God's spiritual revivals as follows:

Bible Study and Personal Review Questions
1. Botanically, what are the three major conditions necessary for seed germination?
2. What additional germination requirements are needed by some other seeds before they can germinate?
3. In what practical ways are revivals comparable to the germination of seeds?
4. Can any seeds germinate without the conditions for their germination being provided?
5. Similarly, can any revivals be granted by God without the practical conditions for their outpouring being provided?

1. REVIVALS ARE GRANTED ONLY WHEN WE ARE PREPARED TO COME OUT OF OUR SPIRITUAL LUKEWARMNESS AND SPIRITUAL COLDNESS

Spiritual lukewarmness which always leads to spiritual coldness are the two unfortunate spiritual conditions which depict our spiritual degradation and always ring the bell on our need for God's spiritual revivals and spiritual renewals. Spiritual lukewarmness is the spiritual condition of neither being very interested nor very enthusiastic about the Holy God and His holy values and standards for His genuine children and faithful followers.

When lukewarmness leads you to lower your standard, commitment and attachment to God this way and you still remain in the church physically doing what you were formerly doing but spiritually without any fervour or passion for Christ as well as His ethical values and standards of spiritual efficiency, then the Bible describes you as being neither hot nor cold which condition is always the first step towards total spiritual backsliding for all His sincere children and followers.

So whenever you sense this spiritual retrogression and you keep quiet, then you are digging your own spiritual grave and further making a public announcement that you are soon going to die spiritually! It is for this reason that the Bible exhorts us strongly to avoid spiritual lukewarmness totally in the following Bible references:

Matthew 7:16-17

You will know them by their fruits. Do men gather grapes from thornbushes or figs from thistles? Even so, every good tree bears good fruit, but a bad tree bears bad fruit. NKJV

Isaiah 29:13

Therefore the Lord said: "Inasmuch as these people draw near with their mouths and honor Me with their lips, but have removed their hearts far from Me, and their fear toward Me is taught by the commandment of men." NKJV

Titus 1:16

They profess to know God, but in works they deny Him, being abominable, disobedient, and disqualified for every good work. NKJV

According to the Cambridge dictionary, apathy is the behaviour that shows no interest or energy and shows that someone is unwilling to take action, especially over something important. According to this definition, the exhibition of apathy has two facets. The first one concerns the lack or loss of interest in something like spiritual renewals which are very important. The second one is the total refusal to do anything meaningful and beneficial about this thing and allow things to be destroyed without showing any concerns or bringing in any interventions to arrest the downward trend of affairs.

The amazing thing about the church in Laodicea was not the fact that there were visible signs of spiritual retrogression in their fold, but that they remained so unconcerned and apathetic about this sad spiritual condition as mentioned in the passage quoted below as follows:

<u>Revelation 3:15a, 17</u>
I know your works, that you are neither cold nor hot. Because you say, I am rich, have become wealthy, and have need of nothing' — and do not know that you are wretched, miserable, poor, blind, and naked. NKJV

We go to the hospital only when we are sick because that is the place where we are sure that we can get qualified Doctors and Physicians to examine us and prescribe the appropriate drugs and remedies which can cure our sicknesses. In the same way, the first major condition of revival which God looks out for before He pours it on an individual or upon the church is the setting aside of our spiritual apathy towards our pitiable spiritual condition of total spiritual lukewarmness and spiritual coldness, and admitting that we are spiritually sick and therefore in urgent need of God's special spiritual rekindling to prevent our total spiritual death. Failure to do this can lead us to perpetual spiritual coldness and in extreme cases even into total spiritual backsliding as we read in the following passage about the Church in Sardis.

<u>Revelation 3:1-3a</u>
"And to the angel of the church in Sardis write, 'These things says He who has the seven Spirits of God and the seven stars: "I know your works, that you have a name that you are alive, but you are dead. Be watchful, and strengthen the things which remain, that are ready to die, for I have not found your works perfect before God. Remember therefore how you have received and heard; hold fast and repent. NKJV

If we truly desire God's regular revivals today as a Church, then our prayer towards all forms of lukewarmness should be similar to the prayers offered in Lamentations 5:21 and Habakkuk 3:2 as follows: *"Turn us back to You, O Lord, and we will be restored; renew our days as of old."* NKJV, *"O Lord, I have heard Your speech and was afraid; O Lord, revive Your work in the midst of the years! In the midst of the years make it known; in wrath remember mercy."* NKJV. This will make God visit us with the needed spiritual revivals and renewals.

The final reminder is this. We can receive God's regular spiritual revivals only when we realize our spiritual condition of lukewarmness and coldness as mentioned above and are prepared to cast aside any forms of false complacency, apathy and useless spiritual arrogance in order to be able to cry unto God for immediate intervention with His revival fire. As we cry to God for such a divine intervention in our spiritual chaos, we should be specific to cry unto Him until He grants us the following important spiritual interventions to start a new process of revival and renewal in us for us to be able to continue with Him. The details are as follows:

A. To bring us back unto Himself

We need this revival because we have strayed from God into lukewarmness and into the state of spiritual death whose direct consequences are total spiritual rejection by God. 2 Chronicles 7:14 says, *"If My people who are called by My name will humble themselves, and pray and seek My face, and turn from their wicked ways, then I will hear from heaven, and will forgive their sin and heal their land."* NKJV

B. To rekindle our Spiritual passion

In this state, God's revival is needed to reignite in us a new passion and love for God and His purposes. True revival whenever it is sought takes us out of spiritual dryness. Revelation 2:4-5 says, *"Nevertheless I have this against you, that you have left your first love. Remember therefore from where you have fallen; repent and do the first works, or else I will come to you quickly and remove your lampstand from its place – unless you repent."* NKJV

C. **To bring us a new spiritual transformation**

All true revivals can spiritually be contagious because it might start as a personal renewal but can also spiritually transform churches and communities and even spread nationwide. In Acts 2, when the Holy Spirit was poured out on the Day of Pentecost, the disciples were only 120 but the fire spread out from them resulting in the conversion of thousands of people and the birth of the early Church. Revival is needed because it brings us back to God and restores our spiritual passion.

Acts 2:41

Then those who gladly received his word were baptized; and that day about three thousand souls were added to them. NKJV

Acts 4:4

However, many of those who heard the word believed; and the number of the men came to be about five thousand. NKJV

D. To renew us in service for God

Our spiritual fervour sometimes needs a major boost to help us work assiduously towards the fulfilment of the Great Commission in Matthew 28:19-20. Before we can work continually to help fulfill the Great Commission, we need God's constant and regular spiritual revivals to give us renewed strength.

Matthew 28:18-20

And Jesus came and spoke to them, saying, "All authority has been given to Me in heaven and on earth. Go therefore and make disciples of all the nations, baptizing them in the name of the Father and of the Son and of the Holy Spirit, teaching them to observe all things that I have commanded you; and lo, I am with you always, even to the end of the age." Amen. NKJV

Bible Study and Personal Review Questions
1. What is spiritual lukewarmness? How can you explain it in your own words?
2. What is spiritual coldness? How can it also be explained very well to the ordinary Christian?

3. What relationship do spiritual lukewarmness and spiritual coldness have with our search for God's spiritual revival and spiritual renewal.

4. What is the best attitude to adopt towards spiritual lukewarmness and spiritual coldness if we are serious to obtain God's spiritual revival?

5. What is apathy? How can it work against our being able to receive God's spiritual revivals and renewals regularly?

6. What is the first practical condition relating to spiritual coldness and spiritual lukewarmness which we must meet before we can experience God's revival?

7. Anytime we sense spiritual coldness and spiritual lukewarmness in our lives, what message, spiritual edge and practical action should this bring to us?

8. What are some of the important reasons provided here for which we should always discard spiritual lukewarmness and spiritual coldness and always desire and seek God's spiritual revival and spiritual renewal?

9. What was the major mistake of the ancient churches mentioned in connection with their spiritual lukewarmness and spiritual coldness?

10. Are many individual Christians and Christian churches not exhibiting the same level of spiritual apathy they also exhibited in spite of their

lukewarmness and backsliding? What can be done about this immediately?

2. **REVIVALS ARE GRANTED ONLY WHEN WE INTENSELY DESIRE THEM IN OUR HEARTS, IN OUR LIVES AND IN THE CHURCH**

The great truth about revival must be emphasized and reemphasized several times that there can never be any revival in our personal lives and churches until we come to the point where we realize that we genuinely and intensely need and desire it. Many people talk about revivals and become part of revival programmes to hypocritically create a false outward impression that they have a genuine hunger and desire for God's revival when in their heart of hearts, they are only performing a false outward show.

If the many Christians who are in the world today had a genuine and burning desire for God's revival, we could have transformed the world several times over for the Lord Jesus Christ by now. But the word, "revival" has become a cliché in the church of Christ today. We talk about it and preach about it but because it has become commonplace, it has lost its impact upon us and has no serious meaning for us. A cliché is a word, phrase or opinion that is so overused that it has lost its original meaning and impact. This attitude of many Christians towards revivals in the church of

Christ today is comparable to feigning to drink water when you are not thirsty and trying to eat food when you do not feel any hunger at all. With the lack of genuine thirst and hunger, how far can you go in these two exercises?

Every church in the world occasionally talks about revival. But how many of these churches genuinely desire and are ready to work for the fire of the Holy Spirit to start burning in them, in their leaders, and in their individual members continually to enable the church make a great spiritual impact for Christ in this end-time period? The desire for revival such as the early disciples had which encouraged them to pray continually in the upper room for about 40 days to be able to receive the promise of the Father is lacking in the Church today (Luke 24:49).

Luke 24:49
Behold, I send the Promise of My Father upon you; but tarry in the city of Jerusalem until you are endued with power from on high. NKJV

The open truth today is that in many churches, the genuine and intense desire for regular personal and corporate revivals is neither encouraged nor emphasized. Consequently, they are non-existent. To help us to correct this, let us look at the genuine thirst and hunger expressed by some of the great saints in the Scriptures before they could be fully revived to make any meaningful impact for God.

Psalm 51:10

Create in me a clean heart, O God, and renew a steadfast spirit within me. NKJV

Psalm 119:20

My soul breaks with longing for Your judgments at all times. NKJV

Isaiah 26:9

With my soul I have desired You in the night, yes, by my spirit within me I will seek You early; for when Your judgments are in the earth, the inhabitants of the world will learn righteousness. NKJV

Psalm 119:81

My soul faints for Your salvation, but I hope in Your word. NKJV

Psalm 42:2

My soul thirsts for God, for the living God. When shall I come and appear before God? NKJV

In all the references quoted above, there is a clear expression of intense desire for God's presence, revival and renewal. In the first reference, the Psalmist said, "renew a steadfast spirit within me." In Psalm 119:20, the Psalmist said, "My soul breaks with longing for Your judgments." Isaiah 26:9 says, "With my soul I have desired You in the night, yes, by my spirit within me I will seek You early." Psalm 119:81 says, "My soul faints for Your salvation." Psalm 42:2 says, "My soul thirsts for God, for the living God." Though different metaphors and comparisons are used in all the references, the intense desire for God and for His revival and renewal are clearly and emphatically expressed in all of them. Do we have a similar desire for God and for His regular spiritual revivals today?

We are more concerned about social programmes and activities which will please the world more than pursuing revival programmes which will create a longing in us for God's spiritual revival, renewal and restoration. Let us at this juncture go through a list of some of the pertinent reasons why we must all have intense desire for God's revival in our churches today. The intention is to portray with clear practical evidence that things are not what they should be in the church today to promote and bring regular spiritual elevation to us at the personal and general church level. Some of the specific reasons are as follows:

SOME PRACTICAL REASONS WHY WE SHOULD HAVE INTENSE DESIRE FOR GOD AND HIS REVIVALS IN THE CHURCH TODAY

i. Sincerely, we need revival in the church today because our love for Him which led to our firm commitment to Him and His values has gone down tremendously.

    <u>Revelation 2:4, 5</u>
    Nevertheless I have this against you, that you have left your first love. Remember therefore from where you have fallen; repent and do the first works, or else I will come to you quickly and remove your lampstand from its place – unless you repent. NKJV

ii. We need revival because material occupations and worldly concerns are more important to us today than the pursuit of God's true eternal values.

    <u>Titus 2:11, 12</u>
    For the grace of God that brings salvation has appeared to all men, teaching us that, denying ungodliness and worldly lusts, we should live soberly, righteously, and godly in the present age. NKJV

<u>Matthew 16:26</u>
For what profit is it to a man if he gains the whole world, and loses his own soul? Or what will a man give in exchange for his soul? NKJV

iii. We need revival because we spend more time scrolling through the social media than reading the Bible, praying regularly, doing God's work and doing His biddings.

<u>Ephesians 5:11</u>
And have no fellowship with the unfruitful works of darkness, but rather expose them. NKJV

<u>Psalm 1:1, 2</u>
Blessed is the man who walks not in the counsel of the ungodly, nor stands in the path of sinners, nor sits in the seat of the scornful; but his delight is in the law of the Lord, and in His law he meditates day and night. NKJV

iv. We need revival because church parties, empty social programmes, and other feasting programmes receive a greater attendance than prayer meetings and revival programmes no matter how well they are advertised and organized.

<u>1 Peter 4:3</u>
For we have spent enough of our past lifetime in doing the will of the Gentiles – when we walked in lewdness, lusts,

*drunkenness, revelries, drinking parties, and abominable
idolatries.* NKJV

<u>Galatians 5:21</u>
*Envy, murders, drunkenness, revelries, and the like; of
which I tell you beforehand, just as I also told you in time
past, that those who practice such things will not inherit
the kingdom of God.* NKJV

v. Surely, we need revival because we are so
preoccupied with the things of the world that we
have little or no time and desire for consistent
personal prayer and involvement in activities which
have a direct bearing on our spiritual future.

<u>1 John 2:15-17</u>
*Do not love the world or the things in the world. If anyone
loves the world, the love of the Father is not in him. For all
that is in the world — the lust of the flesh, the lust of the
eyes, and the pride of life — is not of the Father but is of the
world. And the world is passing away, and the lust of it;
but he who does the will of God abides forever.* NKJV

vi. We need revival because we are more concerned
about making money than faithfully giving money to
support missions, evangelism and other outreach
programmes of the church.

<u>Proverbs 11:24, 25</u>

There is one who scatters, yet increases more; and there is one who withholds more than is right, but it leads to poverty. The generous soul will be made rich, and he who waters will also be watered himself. NKJV

vii. We need urgent revival because we are unable to practice the truth we have been taught in our lives as they touch on commitment to God, morality, spiritual renewal and spiritual restoration.

James 1:22

But be doers of the word, and not hearers only, deceiving yourselves. NKJV

Matthew 7:24

"Therefore whoever hears these sayings of Mine, and does them, I will liken him to a wise man who built his house on the rock. NKJV

viii. We need revival because we feel shy to share the gospel with, and to talk to others about what has not become real and practicable in our own lives ever since we claimed to have seen Jesus.

Matthew 10:32-33

"Therefore whoever confesses Me before men, him I will also confess before My Father who is in heaven. But whoever denies Me before men, him I will also deny before My Father who is in heaven. NKJV

<u>1 Peter 3:15-16</u>
But sanctify the Lord God in your hearts, and always be ready to give a defense to everyone who asks you a reason for the hope that is in you, with meekness and fear; having a good conscience, that when they defame you as evildoers, those who revile your good conduct in Christ may be ashamed. NKJV

ix. We need revival because we have more time for sports, football, worldly recreation and entertainment than for Bible study, prayer and other devotional and spiritual activities which will draw us closer to God.

<u>2 Timothy 2:15</u>
Be diligent to present yourself approved to God, a worker who does not need to be ashamed, rightly dividing the word of truth. NKJV

<u>Romans 15:4</u>
For whatever things were written before were written for our learning, that we through the patience and comfort of the Scriptures might have hope. NKJV

<u>Colossians 4:2</u>
Continue earnestly in prayer, being vigilant in it with thanksgiving. NKJV

x. We need revival because we are gradually conforming to the world and its worldly standards instead of the world being influenced by our lives for Christ.

Romans 12:2
And do not be conformed to this world, but be transformed by the renewing of your mind, that you may prove what is that good and acceptable and perfect will of God. NKJV

1 Peter 1:14
As obedient children, not conforming yourselves to the former lusts, as in your ignorance. NKJV

Matthew 5:16
Let your light so shine before men, that they may see your good works and glorify your Father in heaven. NKJV

xi. We need revival because we have become friends of the world contrary to what James 4:4 says.

James 4:4
"Adulterers and adulteresses! Do you not know that friendship with the world is enmity with God? Whoever therefore wants to be a friend of the world makes himself an enemy of God." NKJV

xii. We need revival because of the wanton immorality and sexual deviations in our secret lives in the church today.

1 Corinthians 10:8

Nor let us commit sexual immorality, as some of them did, and in one day twenty-three thousand fell. NKJV

<u>1 Corinthians 6:9</u>
Do you not know that the unrighteous will not inherit the kingdom of God? Do not be deceived. Neither fornicators, nor idolaters, nor adulterers, nor homosexuals, nor sodomites. NKJV

xiii. We need revival because the burning fire of the Holy Spirit is no more burning in our hearts, in our lives and in our churches because of prayerlessness and some of the reasons listed above which have exposed us to spiritism and demonism.

<u>Acts 2:3-4</u>
Then there appeared to them divided tongues, as of fire, and one sat upon each of them. And they were all filled with the Holy Spirit and began to speak with other tongues, as the Spirit gave them utterance. NKJV

<u>Psalm 97:3</u>
A fire goes before Him, and burns up His enemies round about. NKJV

xiv. We need revival because there is evidence from all angles that there is serious lukewarmness in our lives which Christ seriously detests in the lives of all His true children.

<u>*Revelation 3:15, 16*</u>

"I know your works, that you are neither cold nor hot. I could wish you were cold or hot. So then, because you are lukewarm, and neither cold nor hot, I will vomit you out of My mouth. NKJV

xv. We need revival because it can be asserted from what is going on around us in the church today that a lot of spiritual leaders and church members who were formerly on fire for Christ can now be categorized as spiritually dead believers.

<u>Colossians 2:13</u>

And you, being dead in your trespasses and the uncircumcision of your flesh, He has made alive together with Him, having forgiven you all trespasses. NKJV

<u>Ephesians 5:8</u>

For you were once darkness, but now you are light in the Lord. Walk as children of light. NKJV

xvi. We need revival because many churches are only paying lip service to revival and true spiritual renewals as well as the desire to seek it without seriously doing anything practical to attain these spiritual ideals.

<u>Matthew 15:8</u>

"'These people honor me with their lips, but their hearts are far from me." NIV

<u>Isaiah 29:13, 14</u>

The Lord says: "These people come near to me with their mouth and honor me with their lips, but their hearts are far from me. Their worship of me is based on merely human rules they have been taught. Therefore once more I will astound these people with wonder upon wonder; the wisdom of the wise will perish, the intelligence of the intelligent will vanish." NIV

xvii. The conclusion to the whole matter is that we need revival seriously and urgently because spiritually, practically and socially we are in a big trouble! Let us therefore generate the desire which can lead us to seek and obtain God's spiritual revivals and spiritual renewals immediately with the words from Psalm 85:6 and Psalm 80:19 which together read: *"**Will You not revive us again, that Your people may rejoice in You**?"* (Psalm 85:6) "**Restore us, O Lord God of hosts; cause Your face to shine, and we shall be saved!**" (Psalm 80:19) NKJV

Bible Study and Personal Review Questions

1. Will you agree with the statement that God can never grant us any spiritual revivals until He sees a genuine and intense desire for them in our hearts?

2. Why does God first look at the heart before granting us His spiritual revivals and not only at our involvement in Church activities?

3. To what level have the words, "revival and renewal" been reduced in the Church of the Lord Jesus Christ today?

4. What is the importance of genuine thirst to our drinking water and of genuine hunger to our eating food? Without the existence of these two human desires, can water and food be consumed satisfactorily?

5. In the same way, can God grant us any personal and corporate revivals in the Church if we do not have any intense and burning desire for them in our hearts?

6. What hypocrisy is the contemporary church of Christ exhibiting towards genuine spiritual revivals and spiritual renewals today?

7. What expressions of genuine and intense desire for God and His spiritual renewals do we have in the references quoted as follows: (Luke 24:49; Psalm 51:10; Psalm 119:20; Isaiah 26:9; Psalm 119:81; Psalm 42:2)

8. What are some of the practical proofs listed and outlined here which clearly establish that our present generation and its numerous peoples do not sincerely and intensely desire God's spiritual revivals and renewals as we read in the references quoted in the previous question?

9. What urgent prayer for both personal and corporate revival should we address to God as individual Christians and as a Church?

3. REVIVALS ARE GRANTED ONLY WHEN WE ARE PREPARED TO PAY THE PRICE FOR THEM TO COME

There is always a cost attached to every good and important thing in life whether it is spiritual or physical. We can therefore conclude that in our created world, nothing happens for nothing and nothing is attained or achieved for nothing. Many people are cold and lukewarm in the Church of the Lord Jesus Christ today not because Christ is not willing to revive, strengthen and empower them but simply because they are not ready and fully prepared to pay the price attached to this desire for God's revival. If the Holy Spirit can gloss over all the necessary conditions for revival, at least there are two of them which are totally unavoidable. These are self-denial and perseverance. We will start with self-denial. What is self-denial and how is it connected with God's revivals?

Self-denial is the willingness to go without certain comforts in life to make it possible for you to attain your desired goals. Self-denial is always necessary before you can begin the Christian life and walk with

Christ successfully. It is also totally indispensable in our search for God's spiritual revivals and renewals. Because the desire for urgent revival is non-existent in the hearts of many Christians today, the desire to practice self-denial to be able to receive and maintain this revival regularly is also non-existent. Apart from doing away with the list of revival killers which is presented in the preceding major sub-section 2 above under "SOME PRACTICAL REASONS WHY WE SHOULD HAVE INTENSE DESIRE FOR GOD AND HIS REVIVALS IN THE CHURCH TODAY", receiving God's revivals will also surely demand a certain high level of self-denial on our part.

Let us consider the following biblical references on self-denial and self-renunciation to help us:

Matthew 16:24
Then Jesus said to His disciples, "If anyone desires to come after Me, let him deny himself, and take up his cross, and follow Me. NKJV

1 Peter 2:11
Beloved, I beg you as sojourners and pilgrims, abstain from fleshly lusts which war against the soul. NKJV

<u>Daniel 1:8</u>

But Daniel purposed in his heart that he would not defile himself with the portion of the king's delicacies, nor with the wine which he drank; therefore he requested of the chief of the eunuchs that he might not defile himself. NKJV

<u>Hebrews 11:24-26</u>

By faith Moses, when he became of age, refused to be called the son of Pharaoh's daughter, choosing rather to suffer affliction with the people of God than to enjoy the passing pleasures of sin, esteeming the reproach of Christ greater riches than the treasures in Egypt; for he looked to the reward. NKJV

Apart from practicing self-denial which can lead us into taking up our cross to be able to follow Jesus, self-denial is also required to enable us to shun sin and to walk in holiness and purity which is an important precondition for God's revival.

The second important attitude which we want to discuss in relation to the cost of revival is the attitude of perseverance and persistence. To persist in doing something is to be firm and resolute in the face of great challenges. To persevere therefore is to continue to move on and to continue to press on towards your goal in defiance of all the obstacles, problems and major hindrances which can come your way. This attitude is extremely necessary when seeking God's spiritual revival.

Because the Bible has not set any timelines for the granting of God's revivals, the search for God's revival can come immediately, after some short time or after a long period of preparation and prayer. So depending upon the state of your heart and your level of spiritual and practical preparation, the response to your prayer for revival could take either a short or long time. If you do not have persistence and a persevering spirit, you will give up before the revival dawns and miss God's grace in your spiritual elevation.

Let us never forget that the 120 disciples who met in the upper room had to walk with Jesus to receive His teachings for about three years and further give themselves to continuous prayer for about 40 days before the tongues of fire came to settle upon them to empower them for ministry. If they had given up before this time, what would have happened? So we need perseverance at all the important levels before we can secure and maintain God's revivals. Let us consider the following Scriptures which emphasize the importance of perseverance and persistence.

Luke 11:9-10

"So I say to you, ask, and it will be given to you; seek, and you will find; knock, and it will be opened to you. For everyone who asks receives, and he who seeks finds, and to him who knocks it will be opened. NKJV

Luke 18:1

Then He spoke a parable to them, that men always ought to pray and not lose heart. NKJV

Bible Study and Personal Review Questions
1. Is it true to make the claim that there is a cost attached to every good thing in life both physical and spiritual?
2. In connection with this, why are so many people still lacking God's revivals in the Church of Christ when they sincerely need this spiritual grace?
3. What are the two important spiritual attitudes which are totally unavoidable in our search for God's revivals?
4. What is self-denial? Practically, how can it help us to secure God's revival?
5. What is perseverance? How can its availability help us to secure and maintain God's revival?

6. What is perseverance? What is its importance in our search for God's revivals?

4. REVIVALS ARE GRANTED ONLY WHEN GOD GETS THE RIGHT CHANNELS TO USE

The greatest hindrance to the outpouring of God's revival has always been sin! Sin is always committed by individuals and groups of persons in the church. Sin has always been the devil's greatest tool to cause backsliding and the destruction of God's burning fire in His church. This explains why every genuine revival must always begin with genuine repentance and a forsaking of all known sins. We can desire revival for years but if the church does not provide the appropriate human channels who can be used by God, this desire will always remain elusive.

So the first step towards any genuine personal or group revivals in the church is self-examination and hard searching leading to sincere repentance and a total renunciation of all sins. This is the act which ultimately leads to cleansing, spiritual renewal and spiritual restoration. The Spirit of God is able to effect this in the local church for God's revivals to begin only when He gets the right channels who have not soiled their holy garments with sin to use to announce and encourage this return to Him as He used Hulda to do in the illustrative passage quoted below as follows:

2 Chronicles 34:23-33

She said to them, "This is what the Lord, the God of Israel, says: Tell the man who sent you to me, 'This is what the Lord says: I am going to bring disaster on this place and its people — all the curses written in the book that has been read in the presence of the king of Judah. Because they have forsaken me and burned incense to other gods and aroused my anger by all that their hands have made, my anger will be poured out on this place and will not be quenched.' Tell the king of Judah, who sent you to inquire of the Lord, 'This is what the Lord, the God of Israel, says concerning the words you heard: Because your heart was responsive and you humbled yourself before God when you heard what he spoke against this place and its people, and because you humbled yourself before me and tore your robes and wept in my presence, I have heard you, declares the Lord. Now I will gather you to your ancestors, and you will be buried in peace. Your eyes will not see all the disaster I am going to bring on this place and on those who live here.'" So they took her answer back to the king.

Then the king called together all the elders of Judah and Jerusalem. He went up to the temple of the Lord with the people of Judah, the inhabitants of Jerusalem, the priests and the Levites – all the people from the least to the greatest. He read in their hearing all the words of the Book of the Covenant, which had been found in the temple of the Lord. The king stood by his pillar and renewed the covenant in the presence of the Lord – to follow the Lord and keep his commands, statutes and decrees with all his heart and all his soul, and to obey the words of the covenant written in this book. Then he had everyone in Jerusalem and Benjamin pledge themselves to it; the people of Jerusalem did this in accordance with the covenant of God, the God of their ancestors. Josiah removed all the detestable idols from all the territory belonging to the Israelites, and he had all who were present in Israel serve the Lord their God. As long as he lived, they did not fail to follow the Lord, the God of their ancestors. NIV

God's holy nation was in need of a deliverer and a saviour like Hulda. The spiritual decline in the land was serious and terrible. All the people had forsaken Jehovah God making them vulnerable to the attacks of their enemies. Their spiritual condition can be described as very chaotic. The same thing happens in the church when through sin and backsliding we lose

God's manifest presence, power, and spiritual revival. But for God to do something positive about such a level of spiritual degradation whenever it occurs, he always needs a holy channel or vessel he can use to announce his intentions to be able to bring back His full presence and power.

As we learn from the passage above, He got this holy channel in the person of Hulda the prophetess who could be used to proclaim God's word to bring everyone back to repentance and a restoration of fellowship with God. Backed by God, her message was so powerful that it brought immediate change and great spiritual revival which affected the king and all the men and women in the kingdom. The revival bore practical proofs because it led to the removal of all the detestable idols from the land and a full return to the law of God.

If we want God's genuine revival in the church today, then we should never forget that God always needs holy channels and vessels who have truly sanctified themselves to become worthy to be used. Throughout the holy Scriptures and throughout the history of the church, God has never brought any revival without initiating this through some sanctified, dedicated and committed vessels like Hulda. In the great revival that occurred to defeat the prophets of Baal, Elijah was God's channel.

In the great revival which gave birth to the New Testament Church, the 120 people who came to pray in the upper room became God's channels and vessels of His power. When God's servants leading the crusade for God's revival start on the right note by emphasizing repentance before revival, God can always get some sanctified vessels through this. Bible passages which can help us to do this effectively include the following quoted below:

<u>Proverbs 28:13</u>
He who covers his sins will not prosper, but whoever confesses and forsakes them will have mercy. NKJV

<u>Psalm 32:5</u>
I acknowledged my sin to You, and my iniquity I have not hidden. I said, "I will confess my transgressions to the Lord," and You forgave the iniquity of my sin. NKJV

<u>Isaiah 59:2</u>
But your iniquities have separated you from your God; and your sins have hidden His face from you, so that He will not hear. NKJV

<u>Psalm 51:10</u>
*Create in me a clean heart, O God, and renew a
steadfast spirit within me.* NKJV

GETTING SANCTIFIED AND COMMITTED HUMAN CHANNELS FOR GOD'S REGULAR REVIVALS IN THE CHURCH TODAY

Judah was lucky to get a sanctified human channel in the person of Hulda to be used to bring them back to repentance and revival. Where can we also get similar sanctified vessels in the church of the Lord Jesus Christ today? As we have just seen, if Hulda became God's channel for the spiritual revival and renewal which broke out during her time through her faithfulness and firm commitment to her God, where are the similar faithful channels in the church today who can also be used mightily by God?

The channels for God's spiritual revivals in the church today are within the Church. They are the local pastors and other men and women gifted in the church as evangelists, teachers, prophets, apostles and so on. These people form the first level of God's channels of revival in the local church. Messages on the importance of God's revival and the need for the entire local church to seek this regularly using books and materials on this subject like the content of this book can regularly teach lessons on God's revivals and how to obtain and maintain them to conscientize the believers and create the desire in them to seek both personal and group revivals. If the church has additional leaders like elders, overseers and tent-making workers, they can all do what can make them holy channels of God's mighty revivals and spiritual renewals.

Other elected and appointed lay leaders like the leaders of the men, women and youth groups can also become effective channels of God's revivals in the church. Additionally, some of the dedicated ordinary church members who are willing can be engaged to pray regularly for God's spiritual revival and renewal (additional details of this are supplied in the subsequent chapters of this book)

PICTURE LESSONS ON GOD'S SPIRITUAL REVIVALS TODAY
Before we conclude our discussion on the channels of God's revivals, let us briefly mention some of the important lessons this episode in Judah teaches us about all of God's revivals as follows:

First, we learn that every true revival from God begins with genuine repentance. Repentance is the realization of our sin and backsliding leading to the desire to have an immediate change of mind and to return fully to God. This happened in the revival in Judah under Hulda. We read about this from the portion of the passage which says:

> *Tell the king of Judah, who sent you to inquire of the Lord, 'This is what the Lord, the God of Israel, says concerning the words you heard: Because your heart was responsive and you humbled yourself before God when you heard what he spoke against this place and its people, and because you humbled yourself before me and tore your robes and wept in my presence, I have heard you, declares the Lord. Now I will gather you to your ancestors, and you will be buried in peace. Your eyes will not see all the disaster I am going to bring on this place and on those who live here.'" So they took her answer back to the king.* NIV (2 Chronicles 34:26-28)

Secondly, this episode teaches us another important lesson about all God-given revivals on restitution. Restitution always comes after repentance and mainly involves confession and putting things right again to make our continuous walk with God possible. It is in the light of this that the Oxford dictionary defines restitution as a recompense for injury or loss. It could also involve many practical things which include throwing away abominable things hated by God as well as the total abandonment of sin and all sinful practices and objects. The Israelites did this in the passage below as follows:

> *Josiah removed all the detestable idols from all the territory belonging to the Israelites, and he had all who were present in Israel serve the Lord their God. As long as he lived, they did not fail to follow the Lord, the God of their ancestors.* NIV (2 Chronicles 34:33a)

Thirdly, we learn from the passage that every true revival from God always culminates in a whole-hearted return to Him and to His former good and profitable ways. This also occurred in the passage as we read as follows:

> *"The king stood by his pillar and renewed the covenant in the presence of the Lord – to follow the Lord and keep his commands, statutes and decrees with all his heart and all his soul, and to obey the words of the covenant written in this book. Then he had everyone in Jerusalem and Benjamin pledge themselves to it; the people of Jerusalem did this in accordance with the covenant of God, the God of their ancestors."* NIV (2 Chronicles 34:31, 32)

> *"As long as he lived, they did not fail to follow the Lord, the God of their ancestors."* NIV (2 Chronicles 34:33b)

To conclude, let me reiterate that it is important to keep this picture lesson in mind as we move to the next chapter of this book on the importance of repentance to our being able to receive and maintain God's revivals regularly.

Bible Study and Personal Review Questions
1. What is the one great enemy of God's revivals?
2. Whenever sin gets hold of church members, what happens to this church eventually?
3. Is God's call on all church members and the entire church to repent before He pours down His revival justifiable? What are the reasons for your answer?
4. What does God often do to arouse the members of a church to this responsibility before pouring down His revival fire?
5. How does the condition of Judah as portrayed in the passage quoted from 2 Chronicles 34:23-33 before Hulda's prophecy reveal the destructive nature of sin whenever it is given a seat among God's people and in the church?
6. When we talk about the need for sanctified spirit-filled channels before any revival, how should we

understand this? What value does this add to all God-given revivals?

7. Which personality became God's special channel in the revival which came to Judah as quoted in the passage under discussion? How well did she perform her task as a spiritual channel to help bring down God's revival?

8. Where can we get similar channels in the church today to help us receive and maintain God's revivals regularly?

9. Why are channels like Hulda still necessary in the church before we can receive God's revival? What exactly can their ministry bring to bear upon God's revivals?

10. What picture does the passage under consideration give us on the three important steps to take to be able to receive God's revival? What is the first step, what is the second step, and what is the third step?

11. Can any God-given revivals be poured in the church today without the believers meeting these conditions both personally and corporately? What are the proofs from the passage to establish your stand and position?

12. Are you desirous to receive God's revival personally or in your church? If yes, where should you start from? How should you press on progressively? And how should you finally end?

CHAPTER TWO
THE CONDITIONS OF GOD'S REVIVAL (PART 2)

<u>INTRODUCTION</u>

There is no way a woman can conceive and give birth to a baby without first going through the normal biological processes established by God for this to take place. Even Abraham and Sarah known in the Bible as the man and woman of faith had to obey this law before they could give birth to Isaac although they were well advanced in age (Genesis 21:1, 2)!

> <u>Genesis 21:1, 2</u>
> *And the Lord visited Sarah as He had said, and the Lord did for Sarah as He had spoken. For Sarah conceived and bore Abraham a son in his old age, at the set time of which God had spoken to him.* (NKJV)

> <u>Genesis 21:1, 2</u>
> *Now the Lord was gracious to Sarah as he had said, and the Lord did for Sarah what he had promised. Sarah became pregnant and bore a son to Abraham in his old age, at the very time God had promised him.* (NIV)

In the same way, it will be naïve for any pastor, church leader or ordinary Christian to think that revivals can come to them personally or generally to affect the whole church without first meeting all the necessary conditions required for this to occur. It will not and cannot happen! This explains why we want to take time to discuss more of the conditions of revival in this chapter. This will give us the opportunity to exhaust our discussion of all the important conditions required for God's sure revivals to take place. Let us discuss this last set of conditions of revival with the following important details:

1. **We must accept the possibility of Revival**
    Some theologians and sceptical Christians think that revivals belong to the old-time religion and that they cannot be experienced in the church today like the scale the ancients experienced it and benefitted fully from it. If we start seeking God's revival with such a mindset, we will end up in the way we started it without any signs of revival. The God of the Bible has no super Christians and low-grade Christians in any dispensation. This can be proved by the fact that when we go through the Bible all the promises on revival are the same for all dispensations and different church periods.

    Those who experienced God's revivals in the past accepted the possibility of their receiving these revivals based upon some of the important promises of God in the Bible on revivals. So if we walk in their steps we can also receive God's revivals today. This is the positive mind with which we must start seeking God's revivals in the church of the Lord Jesus Christ today based upon scriptural promises such as the following:

<u>2 Chronicles 7:14</u>
If My people who are called by My name will humble themselves, and pray and seek My face, and turn from their wicked ways, then I will hear from heaven, and will forgive their sin and heal their land. NKJV

<u>Jeremiah 33:3</u>
Call to Me, and I will answer you, and show you great and mighty things, which you do not know.' NKJV

<u>Jeremiah 29:13</u>
You will seek me and find me when you seek me with all your heart. NIV

<u>Jeremiah 3:22</u>
"Return, faithless people; I will cure you of backsliding." "Yes, we will come to you, for you are the Lord our God. NIV

<u>Zechariah 10:1</u>

Ask the Lord for rain in the time of the latter rain. The Lord will make flashing clouds; He will give them showers of rain, grass in the field for everyone. NKJV

Bible Study and Personal Review Questions

1. How does the birth of Isaac through the normal biological processes of life prove and establish that God's revivals can never be granted until all the conditions necessary for this are met? (Genesis 21:1, 2)

2. Why is it important to be firm on the possibility of revival before initiating any processes to seek God's revivals in our lives and in the church?

3. What are some of the Bible references which establish that God's revivals can be received by His children at any period in the history of the church?

4. What are some of the common unscriptural reasons which often lead people to be skeptical about receiving God's revival today? What is your personal position on this as you read this book on revival?

5. Can you receive God's personal revival as well as regular revivals in your own local church?

2. We must recognize and go to the source of all Revivals

Where does revival come from? What is the one and only true source of all genuine revivals? The one and only true source of revivals is the Godhead – God the father, God the son and God the Holy Spirit. If you want water to gash out to you in abundance either for irrigation purposes or for domestic use and you do not go to a source of great and abundant water, how can you receive this plentiful water for your intended purposes? It is God who grants revivals with His great and omnipotent power. So if you want His revivals in your life and in your church and you do not go to Him by faith to seek His manifest presence to effect these, you have no other source for the revivals you are seeking. Several Bible passages establish the Godhead as our one and only true and sure source of regular revivals. Such Bible passages include the following:

Isaiah 57:15

For this is what the high and exalted One says – he who lives forever, whose name is holy: "I live in a high and holy place, but also with the one who is contrite and lowly in spirit, to revive the spirit of the lowly and to revive the heart of the contrite. NIV

Psalm 80:18

Then we will not turn away from you; revive us, and we will call on your name. NIV

Bible Study and Personal Review Questions

1. What are some of the sources of abundant water supply for us on earth? Why is it that anytime we go to these sources we always get water?

2. According to the references quoted above in this section, who is the one and only sure source of all the revivals we need in our personal lives and in the church?

3. What are some of the wrong sources Satan can deceive us to turn to for evil and demonic power today?

4. Instead of yielding to this deception and falsehood of Satan, what are some of the specific steps we should take to be able to approach God's throne to receive His continuous revival power and fire?

3. We must apply the acceptable principles for securing God's Revivals

What is the secret of receiving God's continuous revivals unhindered? Revivals are conditioned on some important spiritual principles which must be observed to convince God and the Holy Spirit that we are ready and prepared for their spiritual revivals and renewals. Some of these important principles which are listed for us in 2 Chronicles 7:14 include:

i. Genuinely belonging to God in true salvation and new birth (If my people who are called by my name).

ii. The attitude and posture of humility and submission (will humble themselves)

iii. The attitude of continuous prayer (and pray)

iv. The attitude of patient and persistent waiting (and seek my face)

v. The attitude of repentance, separation and a forsaking of all known sins (and turn from their wicked ways)

It is only when these principles are observed sincerely from the heart that God's mighty hand will be moved to grant us the desired spiritual revival (then I will hear from heaven, and I will forgive their sin) and further grant us all the physical and spiritual blessings which always accompany revivals (and will heal their land).

So we cannot receive God's revivals on our own terms by showing total disregard for these principles. God does not need any revival or renewal from us to fulfil any conditions we will set for Him. We rather need His help both spiritually and physically in this regard. So to convince Him that we are serious and desirous for His special revivals and renewals, we must follow His outlined principles with seriousness and determination and He will move!

Bible Study and Personal Review Questions

1. Why is it important to seek God's revivals continually unhindered? What are the advantages which can come to us when this happens in our Christian lives?
2. What is the first attitude to adopt to receive these unhindered revivals according to 2 Chronicles 7:14?
3. What is the second important attitude to adopt to be able to receive God's revivals unhindered according to 2 Chronicles 7:14?
4. What is the third useful attitude to adopt to be able to receive God's revivals unhindered according to 2 Chronicles 7:14?
5. What is the fourth beneficial attitude to adopt to be able to receive God's revivals unhindered according to 2 Chronicles 7:14?
6. What is the number five good attitude to adopt to be able to receive God's revivals unhindered according to 2 Chronicles 7:14?
7. What are the general rewards which can come to us when we obey all these five principles mentioned above?
8. What steps are you going to take as from today to actualize 2 Chronicles 7:14 in your prayer for God's revival?

4. We must remove all personal obstacles and spiritual hindrances to God's Revival

Personal obstacles and spiritual hindrances are the sinful attitudes which make us appear in God's presence as people who are insincere and not serious at all to qualify to see His grace, spiritual revivals and spiritual renewals. Christians who fall into this category include those who habour secret sins (Luke 8:17) and who are living in hypocrisy and pretence (Titus 1:16).

<u>Luke 8:17</u>
For there is nothing hidden that will not be disclosed, and nothing concealed that will not be known or brought out into the open. NIV

<u>Titus 1:16</u>
They claim to know God, but by their actions they deny him. They are detestuble, disobedient and unfit for doing anything good. NIV

Such Christians also include people who are spiritually in league with Satan and his demons through witchcraft, necromancy, sorcery and other forms of spiritual adultery (Revelation 21:8).

<u>Revelation 21:8</u>
But the cowardly, the unbelieving, the vile, the murderers, the sexually immoral, those who practice

magic arts, the idolaters and all liars — they will be consigned to the fiery lake of burning sulfur. This is the second death." NIV

When we come to stand before God to seek His revivals without first renouncing these sinful attitudes, confessing them and breaking totally with them, the Holy and all-knowing God who knows all the secrets of man's heart cannot grant us any God-given revivals. The biblical reference for this refusal on the part of God can be read from Amos 3:3 without the practical manifestation of Isaiah 55:7 which reads:

<u>Amos 3:3</u>
Do two walk together unless they have agreed to do so? (NIV)

Can two people walk together without agreeing on the direction? (NLT)

<u>Isaiah 55:7</u>
Let the wicked forsake his way, and the unrighteous man his thoughts; let him return to the Lord, and He will have mercy on him; and to our God, for He will abundantly pardon. NKJV

Bible Study and Personal Review Questions

1. What definitions can you give of personal obstacles and spiritual hindrances to God's revivals?
2. What are secret sins? What makes them secret? Where are they normally hidden?
3. What is the sin of hypocrisy and pretence? How does it show in ordinary life situations in the conduct of some Christians?
4. What are witchcraft, spiritism and idolatry? What can be some of their devastating spiritual effects on Christians who get involved in them?
5. Can anybody get involved in these vices and still expect to receive God's revivals regularly?
6. What is the value and importance of Amos 3:3 in situations like these?
7. What is the hope of people who find themselves in these situations with regards to God's revivals?

5. We must recognize the need for spiritual purity before accessing God's power in Revival

All through the pages of the Bible from Genesis to revelation, it is always emphasized that purity must precede God's power. In other words, the life of penitence leading to heartfelt confession of sins and a firm commitment to the principles of righteousness and practical holiness in the Bible are always unavoidable preconditions to our being able to experience God's revival power both at the personal and general church level. This was the reason why as soon as God called Abraham He told him in Genesis 17:1b that,

"I am God Almighty; walk before me faithfully and be blameless" NIV

"I am Almighty God; walk before Me and be blameless." NKJV

"I am God All-Powerful. If you obey me and always do right." CEV

This same principle of purity before power in God's sight is also emphasized in other biblical passages like the following:

Genesis 6:9
This is the genealogy of Noah. Noah was a just man, perfect in his generations. Noah walked with God. NKJV

Matthew 5:48
Therefore you shall be perfect, just as your Father in heaven is perfect. NKJV

Job 1:1

There was a man in the land of Uz, whose name was Job; and that man was blameless and upright, and one who feared God and shunned evil. NKJV

God stood upon the holy spiritual disposition of all the characters mentioned in these passages to bless and show them His favour. So as far as God is concerned and the pouring down of His revival fire is concerned, the principle can never be changed to power before purity but will forever remain purity before power!

We are in a world where holiness and practical holy living are played down in many churches for them to appear to be repulsive and unwanted subjects both to the young and to the old. But God has forever been and will forever be a holy God whose holiness demands that His children also walk in holiness before accessing His power in revival. (Psalm 99:9; 1 Peter 1:15, 16; 2 Timothy 2:22).

Psalm 99:9
Exalt the Lord our God, and worship at His holy hill; for the Lord our God is holy. NKJV

1 Peter 1:15-16

But just as he who called you is holy, so be holy in all you do; for it is written: "Be holy, because I am holy." NKJV

<u>2 Timothy 2:22</u>
Flee also youthful lusts; but pursue righteousness, faith, love, peace with those who call on the Lord out of a pure heart. NKJV

Revival is a return to God from sinfulness, waywardness and backsliding which were caused by sin. So how can we stay in this same sinfulness and pray to God to obtain His spiritual renewal and spiritual new life accompanied by His great power? This is not possible!

Bible Study and Personal Review Questions
1. What is the biblical principle of purity before power? How is it related to our quest for God's spiritual revivals?
2. How was this principle exemplified in the lives of spiritual giants like Abraham, Noah and Job?
3. What are some of the reasons behind this principle as far as God is concerned?
4. In fulfilment of this principle what should we always do at the personal and general church levels

before we come before God to seek His spiritual revivals?

5. Is it possible for anyone to reverse this principle of purity before power in God's sight? What is your personal opinion on this?

6. We must recognize our need for the full Power of the Holy Spirit

Genuine thirst and hunger for the omnipotent power of God often poured upon us as the power of the Holy Spirit is one of the driving forces behind our being able to seek earnestly and to obtain God's revivals. We drink water because there is a thirst in us which calls for it. We eat food regularly because there is a hunger in us which calls for it. The thirst and the hunger which will always lead us to seek God's regular revivals is the fullness and the power of the Holy Spirit which always comes with God's righteousness.

This full power of the Holy Spirit is always necessary and needful at all times in the lives of all individual Christians and in the life and activities of all the true churches of Christ. Without the continuous power of the Holy Spirit, we shall be spiritually weak Christians in spiritually weak churches whose weaknesses can only lead to non-performance. So seeking the fullness of the Spirit of God constantly through regular revivals must be given preeminence over and above every other thing in our personal lives and in the life of the church. Christ emphasized the importance of this at the end of His earthly ministry in Luke 24:49 and Acts 1:8 which gave birth to the first great revival in the church of Christ.

<u>Luke 24:49</u>
I am going to send you what my Father has promised; but stay in the city until you have been clothed with power from on high." NIV

<u>Acts 1:8</u>
But you will receive power when the Holy Spirit comes on you; and you will be my witnesses in Jerusalem, and in all Judea and Samaria, and to the ends of the earth." NIV

Anytime a church or some individual Christians quench the regular revival fire through which the power of the Holy Spirit is imparted regularly, waywardness, backsliding and in extreme cases apostasy set in! So let us keep God's revival fire which brings down the full power and fire of the Holy Spirit burning in our personal lives and in the church of Christ and spiritually and practically all shall be well with us.

Bible Study and Personal Review Questions

1. What relationship exists between the Holy Spirit and God's revivals?

2. Why do we drink water and eat food regularly as human beings?

3. Spiritually what place should the Holy Spirit and His power occupy in our lives like the food we eat and the water we drink?

4. What is the major cause of spiritually weak Christians and spiritually weak churches today? How can our seeking the power of the Holy Spirit in regular revivals help us here?

5. Why did the Lord Jesus Christ not allow His disciples and followers to form any church or to start any ministry until the fulfilment of Luke 24:49?

6. Can we avoid the fullness and power of the Holy Spirit which is often granted through regular revivals in the local church and still survive both spiritually and physically?

7. Will you agree with the assertion that every true revival service and every true personal revival programme must always include special times of prayer for the fullness and power of the Holy Spirit? If yes, why?

7. We must be prepared to seek God's Revival through continuous Prayer.

The only way we can communicate continuously with our living but invisible God is through the prayer of faith. Apart from the Lord Jesus Christ who came down from the very presence of God in heaven, nobody has seen God as He essentially is before. What we know about Him on earth are only theophanies and not as He really is. Moses saw Him as a burning bush. Abraham saw Him as fire coming down to consume his sacrifice. Israel saw Him as fire and smoke on mount Sinai. Israel again saw Him as a pillar of cloud by day and as a pillar of fire by night during the exodus. So the only way we can communicate with Him to receive His blessings such as are envisaged in spiritual revivals is through the prayer of faith by standing upon some of His numerous promises in the Bible!

Just as there is no revival without holiness, there's also no revival without prayer. This is why prayer is included in the principles outlined in 2 Chronicles 7:14. Other Bible passages emphasizing the importance of prayer in our quest for God's revivals can be read as follows:

<u>Psalm 119:88</u>
Revive me according to Your lovingkindness, so that I may keep the testimony of Your mouth. NKJV

<u>Psalm 80:19</u>
*Restore us, O Lord God of hosts; cause Your face to
shine, and we shall be saved!* NKJV

<u>Psalm 85:6</u>
*Will You not revive us again, that Your people may
rejoice in You?* NKJV

Bible Study and Personal Review Questions
1. Is it accurate and justified to claim that there is no
    revival without prayer? What is the biblical basis
    for this claim?
2. If our living God is physically invisible, then what
    is the best way to communicate with Him
    personally and corporately in the church?
3. Why will it not be possible to access God's spiritual
    revivals and renewals without prayer?
4. What are some of the specific spiritual revival and
    spiritual renewal prayers you can address to God
    in times of revival?

8. **We must recognize our need for the full presence of
   the Godhead in our lives and in the church of Christ**
   There is a void and spiritual vacuum in every person
   born of a woman on earth which crave for fulfilment.
   This vacuum is the natural desire for the God who
   created us in His own image and to whom we must be

spiritually responsive and totally dependent. This explains why in societies which have no knowledge about the worship of the one and only true God, people resort to idol worship and the worship of carved and formed images.

There is a natural craving in every man to seek and obtain the full presence of the God who created him to enjoy His fellowship and sweet presence. Revival is one spiritual event which brings down God's omnipresence to us together with His personal and manifest presence. So it must be sought regularly by all serious-minded individuals and all living and vibrant churches. Being in the presence of God constantly can bring us immense benefits as we glean from the following references:

Psalm 16:11
*You will show me the path of life; in Your presence
is fullness of joy; at Your right hand are pleasures
forevermore.* NKJV

Psalm 145:18
*The Lord is near to all who call upon Him, to all who
call upon Him in truth.* NKJV

Deuteronomy 31:6

Be strong and of good courage, do not fear nor be afraid of them; for the Lord your God, He is the One who goes with you. He will not leave you nor forsake you." NKJV

<u>James 4:8</u>
Draw near to God and He will draw near to you. Cleanse your hands, you sinners; and purify your hearts, you double-minded. NKJV

Bible Study and Personal Review Questions
1. Is it true to claim that there is a void and spiritual vacuum in every man born of a woman on earth?
2. What are the reasons for this void and vacuum and how can they be explained?
3. How is this spiritual vacuum sometimes wrongly manifested in false worship?
4. How do God's regular revivals help to bring satisfaction and fulfilment to this void and vacuum in mankind?
5. What is the relationship of revivals to the manifestation of God's three-fold presence?

CHAPTER THREE
GENUINE REPENTANCE AND GOD'S REVIVALS

INTRODUCTION

One of the greatest passages on revival in the Bible is 2 Chronicles 7:14 which reads in full as follows:

> <u>2 Chronicles 7:14</u>
> *If My people who are called by My name will humble themselves, and pray and seek My face, and turn from their wicked ways, then I will hear from heaven, and will forgive their sin and heal their land.*
> NKJV

This passage gives us the three important dimensions of God-given revivals. It clearly emphasizes genuine repentance as the first step to take before we can receive any revivals and renewals from the holy God. *"If My people who are called by My name will humble themselves... and turn from their wicked ways."* After this, it emphasizes prayer as the second important step to take if we truly want to receive God's revivals. *"...and pray and seek My face."* Finally, it mentions God's response in our search for His revivals. It emphasizes this truth in the words, *"...then I will hear from heaven, and will forgive their sin and heal their land."*

Because of the importance of genuine heart-felt repentance to the whole process of revival, let us begin this chapter by examining some scriptural references on this great question of repentance to help us to know THE WHY, THE WHEN, and THE HOW of true repentance that can be accepted by God.

SOME IMPORTANT BIBLE REFERENCES ON GENUINE REPENTANCE

Ephesians 2:1-5

And you He made alive, who were dead in trespasses and sins, in which you once walked according to the course of this world, according to the prince of the power of the air, the spirit who now works in the sons of disobedience, among whom also we all once conducted ourselves in the lusts of our flesh, fulfilling the desires of the flesh and of the mind, and were by nature children of wrath, just as the others. But God, who is rich in mercy, because of His great love with which He loved us, even when we were dead in trespasses, made us alive together with Christ (by grace you have been saved). NKJV

Acts 2:37-38

Now when they heard this, they were cut to the heart, and said to Peter and the rest of the apostles, "Men and brethren, what shall we do?" Then Peter said to them, "Repent, and let every one of you be

baptized in the name of Jesus Christ for the remission of sins; and you shall receive the gift of the Holy Spirit. For the promise is to you and to your children, and to all who are afar off, as many as the Lord our God will call." NKJV

<u>Titus 3:5-6</u>
Not by works of righteousness which we have done, but according to His mercy He saved us, through the washing of regeneration and renewing of the Holy Spirit, whom He poured out on us abundantly through Jesus Christ our Savior. NKJV

To repent according to the Cambridge dictionary is ***to show that you are very sorry for something bad you have done in the past, and wish that you had not done it***. The Oxford Learner's dictionary also gives us another good definition of repentance. It defines repentance as ***the fact of showing that you are sorry for something wrong that you have done.*** Let it be emphasized and reemphasized that as far as God is concerned, ***there is no revival without initial repentance;*** and there can never be any revival anywhere in any church without genuine repentance.

If you do not show sorrow and regret for going wayward which is accompanied by a genuine desire and willingness to turn away from this wicked path, then there is no way God can extend a helping hand to you to lift you out of the deep pit and place you on a level ground. This explains why Apostle Peter commanded his hearers in Acts 3:19 with the words, *"Repent therefore and be converted, that your sins may be blotted out, so that times of refreshing may come from the presence of the Lord."* NKJV

In the passage quoted from Ephesians 2:1-5, a clear line of demarcation is drawn between our former lives as sinners in the world and our present lives as believers. What brought the difference between the former life and the present life was the genuine repentance exhibited which allowed the Holy Spirit to effect the New Birth in us to be able to change our minds, hearts and lives to conform to the new standards of God. If the genuine repentance had not first taken place, the New Life also wouldn't have come. So in the same way, if we want to experience God's revival at any time, and we do not start by repenting of our sins and backsliding, there is no way the blood of Christ can cleanse and purify us to cause us to rise again. Genuine repentance is inevitable in any quest for God and first for his restoration.

Humility always precedes sincere repentance. It is through humility that we are able to realize our helplessness. It is through humility that we are able to accept our sin-guilt. It is through humility that we are able to make open confession of these things to God for forgiveness and cleansing. And finally, it is through this same humility that we are able to submit to God's new standards of purity and righteousness. God's genuine revivals are dying in a lot of churches because of the arrogance with which people sin and justify their sinfulness with lame excuses.

The right humble attitude to show when the word of God comes to us is the attitude the people showed after Peter's sermon in Acts 2:37-38. In humility the hearers asked the question *"Men and brethren, what shall we do?"* Which led Apostle Peter to readily tell them *"Repent, and let every one of you be baptized in the name of Jesus Christ for the remission of sins; and you shall receive the gift of the Holy Spirit. For the promise is to you and to your children, and to all who are afar off, as many as the Lord our God will call."* This explains why Apostle Paul tells us in Titus 3:5-6 that salvation does not come to us out of merit but through our genuine repentance which brings us the regeneration of the Holy Spirit.

Bible Study and Personal Review Questions
1. What are the three important dimensions of God's revivals mentioned in 2 Chronicles 7:14? What is said about repentance in this quotation? Where was this question of revival placed and why?
2. What simple definition does the dictionary give of repentance? What are some of the important practical processes involved on the road to repentance according to Acts 3:19?

3. What is the importance of genuine repentance to our being able to receive the promised blessings in Ephesians 2:1-5?

4. According to Acts 2:37-38 what is the importance of repentance to the remission of sins and the full operation of the Holy Spirit in us?

5. According to Titus 3:5-6 what is the importance of genuine repentance to our salvation and regeneration and thereafter to our regular spiritual revivals?

SOME PRACTICAL EXAMPLES OF THE LINK BETWEEN GENUINE REPENTANCE AND REVIVALS

> <u>1 Samuel 7:5, 6</u>
> *And Samuel said, "Gather all Israel to Mizpah, and I will pray to the Lord for you." So they gathered together at Mizpah, drew water, and poured it out before the Lord. And they fasted that day, and said there, "We have sinned against the Lord." And Samuel judged the children of Israel at Mizpah.* NKJV

Genuine repentance is inseparably linked to God's true revivals. We have a very good example at Mizpah after the Israelites had gone wayward and done what was contrary to God's perfect will. They approached God's holy prophet who led them in a prayer of public repentance accompanied by practical acts of repentance. When God forgave their sins and restored them, his full presence came back to them as it was before. Whenever we swallow our pride and come back to God in true penitence to seek his forgiveness through open confession, he forgives us and above all revives and restores us.

Lamentations 2:19

"Arise, cry out in the night, at the beginning of the watches; pour out your heart like water before the face of the Lord. Lift your hands toward Him for the life of your young children, who faint from hunger at the head of every street." NKJV

When Israel again went wayward and wanted God to return to them with His old omnipotent power, the pathway shown them was through repentance and a show of remorse. This is captured in the quotation above from statements like "Arise, cry out…"; "pour out your heart like water before the face of the Lord."

Ezra 9:10; 10:1

And now, O our God, what shall we say after this? For we have forsaken Your commandments. Now while Ezra was praying, and while he was confessing, weeping, and bowing down before the house of God, a very large assembly of men, women, and children gathered to him from Israel; for the people wept very bitterly. NKJV

There is always an inseparable link between genuine revival and genuine repentance. This is why we keep emphasizing in this chapter that there is no revival without genuine repentance. Once again when Israel forsook God's covenant and drifted away from Him in disobedience and Ezra wanted to bring them back to God, what happened? He started with confession, remorse and regret. When the people of Israel saw their sinfulness, waywardness and rebellion, they also followed Ezra in sincere confession accompanied by the shedding of tears. Repentance and confession always precede any genuine revival from God. But arrogance and self-will always plunge us deeper and deeper into trouble.

Bible Study and Personal Review Questions

1. Why do we make the bold claim that genuine repentance is inseparable from God's revivals according to 1 Samuel 7:5, 6?

2. What does Lamentations 2:19 teach us on the need for genuine repentance before revivals and spiritual restoration?

3. Is it true to claim that there is always an inseparable link between genuine repentance and God-given

revivals according to Ezra 9:10; 10:1? What is the proof in this passage?

CHARACTERISTICS OF THE REPENTANCE WHICH BRINGS DOWN GOD'S REVIVAL

1. Conviction of Sin

Any repentance which does not begin with true conviction of sin is always short-lived. It is short-lived because it has no deep roots in the heart. So if we want a genuine revival from God and we want to start well with true repentance, then there must be genuine conviction of sin. Conviction of sin is the strong persuasion, acceptance and belief that we are guilty before God on all counts. It is only after accepting our guilt before God in this way that we can genuinely have a change of mind, heart and attitude through repentance. We have a very good picture of true conviction of sin in the parable of the Pharisee and the Republican.

The Pharisee in his self-righteousness did not begin his repentance and confession with any genuine conviction of sin. He started and ended with bragging and placed himself where he was not with an unfortunate comparison. But the attitude of the Publican shows that he began with genuine conviction of sin by accepting his guilt and unworthiness before

God. So the short prayers he offered were more acceptable before God than the display of arrogance and self-righteousness portrayed by the pharisee (Luke 18:9-14). If we want true revival from God, then our repentance must start with genuine conviction of sin. Pictures of conviction of sin can be obtained from the following references:

<u>John 8:3-11</u>

The teachers of the law and the Pharisees brought in a woman caught in adultery. They made her stand before the group and said to Jesus, "Teacher, this woman was caught in the act of adultery. In the Law Moses commanded us to stone such women. Now what do you say?" They were using this question as a trap, in order to have a basis for accusing him. But Jesus bent down and started to write on the ground with his finger. When they kept on questioning him, he straightened up and said to them, "Let any one of you who is without sin be the first to throw a stone at her." Again he stooped down and wrote on the ground. At this, those who heard began to go away one at a time, the older ones first, until only Jesus was left, with the woman still standing there. Jesus straightened up and asked her, "Woman, where are they? Has no one condemned you?" "No one, sir," she said. "Then neither do I condemn you," Jesus declared. "Go now and leave your life of sin." NIV

<u>2 Corinthians 7:9-10</u>

Yet now I am happy, not because you were made sorry, but because your sorrow led you to repentance. For you became sorrowful as God intended and so were not harmed in any way by us. Godly sorrow brings repentance that leads to salvation and leaves no regret, but worldly sorrow brings death. NIV

<u>2 Samuel 12:13</u>

Then David said to Nathan, "I have sinned against the Lord." Nathan replied, "The Lord has taken away your sin. You are not going to die. NIV

<u>Psalm 51:1, 10-12</u>

Have mercy on me, O God, according to your unfailing love; according to your great compassion blot out my transgressions. Create in me a pure heart, O God, and renew a steadfast spirit within me. Do not cast me from your presence or take your Holy Spirit from me. Restore to me the joy of your salvation and grant me a willing spirit, to sustain me. NIV

2. **Demonstration of Contrition for Sin**

Every true repentance apart from beginning with true conviction of sin also shows forth in deep contrition for sin. Contrition is showing a feeling of deep regret for involvement in sin which comes directly out of your admission of guilt. To show regret for something is to have the mind and show expression that you wish you had not done what you did. Whenever we claim to have repented without this show of regret and contrition, we always go back to the same old sins again with the slightest temptation. So repentance which is not accompanied by contrition can always lead us to go back to our vomit easily.

Proverbs 26:11-12

As a dog returns to its vomit, so fools repeat their folly. Do you see a person wise in their own eyes? There is more hope for a fool than for them. NIV

2 Peter 2:22

Of them the proverbs are true: "A dog returns to its vomit," and, "A sow that is washed returns to her wallowing in the mud." NIV

It must always be borne in mind that any repentance which does not go with a show of contrition (deep godly sorrow and humiliation of heart because of sin) is not complete. The Bible emphasizes that God is highly interested in a broken and contrite heart in the process of repentance. Because this is the only way to make sure that we will not go back and commit the same sins over and over again but will rather progress towards righteousness and piety. Let us look at the following passages on the broken and contrite heart as God wants it to accompany our repentance:

Psalm 51:17

My sacrifice, O God, is a broken spirit; a broken and contrite heart you, God, will not despise. NIV

Isaiah 57:15

For this is what the high and exalted One says – he who lives forever, whose name is holy: "I live in a high and holy place, but also with the one who is contrite and lowly in spirit, to revive the spirit of the lowly and to revive the heart of the contrite." NIV

3. Confession of Sins

Proverbs 28:13 says that, *"He who covers his sins will not prosper, but whoever confesses and forsakes them will have mercy."* Based upon this passage, someone has said that the lack of thorough confession of sins to God for cleansing is like hiding live bullets in the body. Unless these "sinful bullets" are removed from the body, whatever you do, you will die spiritually. Because of its importance to genuine repentance, let us try to understand confession. What does it exactly mean?

Confession is telling God openly or privately all the things you have done wrong so that He can forgive, pardon and cleanse you with the blood of the Lord Jesus Christ. Whenever true conviction of sin and genuine contrition for sin begin the process of repentance, confession becomes natural and spontaneous because the sin-guilt has been admitted and the show of remorse and regret which will prevent you from going back to commit these same sins again has occurred. In this, confession becomes comparable to the gathering together of the waste material for it to be moved out of your life completely so that God can replace it with new life and new values.

The Bible is emphatic on the passage quoted from Proverbs 28:13 that whoever tries to cover his sins from God will never prosper. The Good News Translation renders it, *"You will never succeed in life if you try to hide your sins."* This is applicable to all persons who sincerely desire God's revival in their lives. The same passage is quick to exalt confession in the words, *"But whoever confesses and forsakes them will have mercy."* The Good News Translation also renders it as, *"Confess them and give them up; then God will show mercy to you."* Some important lessons on confession – when to do it, how to do it, where to do it, why we should do it – can be learnt from the following episodes:

<u>2 Samuel 12:13</u>

So David said to Nathan, "I have sinned against the Lord." And Nathan said to David, "The Lord also has put away your sin; you shall not die. NKJV

Psalm 51:1

Have mercy upon me, O God, according to Your lovingkindness; according to the multitude of Your tender mercies, blot out my transgressions. NKJV

Luke 15:18-19

I will arise and go to my father, and will say to him, "Father, I have sinned against heaven and before you, and I am no longer worthy to be called your son. Make me like one of your hired servants." NKJV

Luke 18:13-14

And the tax collector, standing afar off, would not so much as raise his eyes to heaven, but beat his breast, saying, 'God, be merciful to me a sinner!' I tell you, this man went down to his house justified rather than the other; for everyone who exalts himself will be humbled, and he who humbles himself will be exalted." NKJV

Psalm 32:1-5

Blessed is he whose transgression is forgiven, whose sin is covered. Blessed is the man to whom the Lord does not impute iniquity, and in whose spirit there is no deceit. When I kept silent, my bones grew old through my groaning all the day long. For day and night Your hand was heavy upon me; my vitality was turned into the drought of summer. I acknowledged my sin to You, and my iniquity I have not hidden. I said, "I will confess my transgressions to the Lord," and You forgave the iniquity of my sin. NKJV

4. Demonstration of New Life in Christ

If revival at any level will start, it will take place only after we have gone through all the three important stages discussed above and have finally agreed to stay and walk in Christ in newness of life in practical holiness and in total purity. We lose our spiritual fire only when we embrace, live with sin and wallow in it. Whenever this happens, because the Spirit of the LORD is holy, and can never stay in dirty vessels, He leaves us and the devil and his demons come to take over and try to plunge us deeper and deeper into sin, waywardness and rebellion.

So when we cry to God from this pitiable condition to show us His mercy and through the process of repentance and confession discussed above He receives us back, washes and cleanses us, we have to stay and walk in newness of life to be able to maintain His revival and restoration both at the individual level and as a corporate church. Bible passages exhorting us to stay and walk in holiness, absolute purity, and New Life include the following:

Five Important Passages on Holy Living after Repentance

<u>1 Thessalonians 4:7</u>
For God did not call us to be impure, but to live a holy life. NIV

<u>Hebrews 12:14</u>
Pursue peace with all people, and holiness, without which no one will see the Lord. NKJV

<u>1 Peter 2:9</u>
But you are a chosen generation, a royal priesthood, a holy nation, His own special people, that you may proclaim the praises of Him who called you out of darkness into His marvelous light. NKJV

<u>Romans 12:1</u>
I beseech you therefore, brethren, by the mercies of God, that you present your bodies a living sacrifice, holy, acceptable to God, which is your reasonable service. NKJV

<u>1 Peter 1:15</u>
But as He who called you is holy, you also be holy in all your conduct. NKJV

Five Important Passages on the New Life in Christ after Genuine Repentance

<u>2 Corinthians 5:17</u>

Therefore, if anyone is in Christ, he is a new creation; old things have passed away; behold, all things have become new. NKJV

<u>Romans 6:4, 11</u>

We were therefore buried with him through baptism into death in order that, just as Christ was raised from the dead through the glory of the Father, we too may live a new life. In the same way, count yourselves dead to sin but alive to God in Christ Jesus. NKJV

<u>Ephesians 4:22-24</u>

You were taught, with regard to your former way of life, to put off your old self, which is being corrupted by its deceitful desires; to be made new in the attitude of your minds; and to put on the new self, created to be like God in true righteousness and holiness. NKJV

<u>Galatians 2:20</u>

I have been crucified with Christ and I no longer live, but Christ lives in me. The life I now live in the body, I live by faith in the Son of God, who loved me and gave himself for me. NKJV

<u>Colossians 3:9-10</u>

Do not lie to each other, since you have taken off your old self with its practices and have put on the new self, which is being renewed in knowledge in the image of its Creator. NKJV

There is always a close affinity between genuine repentance, new life and a life of practical holiness. The reason for this is that true repentance is like a vehicle which conducts us from a bad place of sinfulness against the holy God to a new land of God's holy presence characterized by new life in a new holy kingdom of God whose eternal foundation is holiness. So it cannot truly take place without this form of spiritual motion. There are several proofs of this in the Scriptures such as the following:

1. The repentance in Judah under King Josiah

<u>2 Chronicles 34:24, 25</u>

"Thus says the Lord: 'Behold, I will bring calamity on this place and on its inhabitants, all the curses that are written in the book which they have read before the king of Judah, because they have forsaken Me and burned incense to other gods, that they might provoke Me to anger with all the works of their hands. Therefore My wrath will be poured out on this place, and not be quenched.'" NKJV

2 Chronicles 34:29, 31, 32, 33

Then the king sent and gathered all the elders of Judah and Jerusalem. Then the king stood in his place and made a covenant before the Lord, to follow the Lord, and to keep His commandments and His testimonies and His statutes with all his heart and all his soul, to perform the words of the covenant that were written in this book. And he made all who were present in Jerusalem and Benjamin take a stand. So the inhabitants of Jerusalem did according to the covenant of God, the God of their fathers. Thus Josiah removed all the abominations from all the country that belonged to the children of Israel, and made all who were present in Israel diligently serve the Lord their God. All his days they did not depart from following the Lord God of their fathers. NKJV

2. The repentance of the Ninevites

Jonah 1:1, 2

Now the word of the Lord came to Jonah the son of Amittai, saying, "Arise, go to Nineveh, that great city, and cry out against it; for their wickedness has come up before Me." NKJV

Jonah 3:5, 10

So the people of Nineveh believed God, proclaimed a fast, and put on sackcloth, from the greatest to the least of them. Then God saw their works, that they turned from their evil way; and God relented from the disaster that He had said He would bring upon them, and He did not do it. NKJV

3. The repentance of Apostle Paul

<u>Acts 9:1-7</u>

Then Saul, still breathing threats and murder against the disciples of the Lord, went to the high priest and asked letters from him to the synagogues of Damascus, so that if he found any who were of the Way, whether men or women, he might bring them bound to Jerusalem. As he journeyed he came near Damascus, and suddenly a light shone around him from heaven. Then he fell to the ground, and heard a voice saying to him, "Saul, Saul, why are you persecuting Me?" And he said, "Who are You, Lord?" Then the Lord said, "I am Jesus, whom you are persecuting. It is hard for you to kick against the goads." So he, trembling and astonished, said, "Lord, what do You want me to do?" Then the Lord said to him, "Arise and go into the city, and you will be told what you must do." And the men who journeyed with him stood speechless, hearing a voice but seeing no one. NKJV

<u>Acts 9:19-22</u>

So when he had received food, he was strengthened. Then Saul spent some days with the disciples at Damascus. Immediately he preached the Christ in the synagogues, that He is the Son of God. Then all who heard were amazed, and said, "Is this not he who destroyed those who called on this name in Jerusalem, and has come here for that purpose, so that he might bring them bound to the chief priests?" But Saul increased all the more in strength, and confounded the Jews who dwelt in Damascus, proving that this Jesus is the Christ. NKJV

Bible Study and Personal Review Questions

1. What is conviction of sin? How can it be explained to the ordinary sinner?
2. What is the importance of genuine conviction of sin to true repentance?
3. What is contrition for sin?
4. What is the danger of repentance without contrition? How can true contrition be expressed before repentance?
5. What is repentance? What are some of the key elements of repentance?
6. What is the value of genuine confession to true repentance?
7. If true confession does not follow genuine repentance, how can this be a major drawback in the process of repentance?
8. Whenever genuine and thorough confession follow repentance, what are some of the benefits this action can bring to the sinner?
9. If our repentance and confession are genuine and sincere as discussed above, what are their immediate practical results in our lives?
10. What relationship exists between new life in Christ and holy living in Christ after genuine repentance?

11. Is it possible for someone to claim to have repented as explained above without any practical results of holiness and new life?

12. What does the word of God say on our New Life in Christ after our repentance?

13. What does the word of God say on our practical holiness after our repentance?

14. What proof do we have in the repentance of the people of Judah under King Josiah that every true repentance always leads to new life and a life of practical holiness?

15. What was the level of wickedness of the people of Nineveh? When they repented of their sins, what did God look at to spare them from judgement? What proof does this provide that every true repentance is naturally followed by a change to new life and practical holiness?

16. Who was Apostle Paul before he went to Damascus? What happened to him on his way to Damascus?

17. What convinced the disciples in Christ in Damascus to accept him as one who is genuinely converted?

SOME OF THE COMMON EVERYDAY SINS WE NEED TO REPENT OF TO PAVE THE WAY FOR GOD'S CONTINUOUS REVIVALS

As far as the Bible is concerned, there cannot be any revival anywhere without genuine heart-felt repentance!

The reasons for this are not difficult to find. The creator God who is the only genuine source of all true revivals is an absolutely Holy God. So He does not come down, settle and work in an environment which is full of sin! This will run counter to His absolutely Holy and true nature which is unchangeable and will remain unchangeable forever throughout all generations. This is why we want to emphasize the truth in this section that if we are serious to seek and receive God's true revivals then we must make a clean breast of all sins both secret and open. Bible references affirming this absolutely holy nature of God include the following:

Leviticus 19:2
"Speak to all the congregation of the children of Israel, and say to them: You shall be holy, for I the Lord your God am holy. NKJV

1 Samuel 2:2
"No one is holy like the Lord, for there is none besides You, nor is there any rock like our God. NKJV

Psalm 99:5
Exalt the Lord our God, and worship at His footstool – He is holy. NKJV

1 Peter 1:15

But as He who called you is holy, you also be holy in all your conduct. NKJV

In the light of God's holiness examined above, the basic spiritual condition behind our quest for God's continuous spiritual revivals can be encapsulated in the statement from Matthew 5:48 which reads: "Therefore you shall be perfect, just as your Father in heaven is perfect." It is only by our continuous striving towards this absolute perfection of God that we can regularly receive and maintain God's revivals in our lives at the personal level and corporately at the general church level. Spiritual declension leading to backsliding and satanic invasion occurs whenever we lose sight of this absolutely holy nature of God and start taking liberties with sin.

So if we want to receive God's spiritual revivals at any time, maintain them and enjoy their fruits then the life of continuous practical holiness is a must. Though it may not be practically possible for us as Christians living with the presence of sin to reach this high level of the absolute perfection of God Himself while on earth, at least there must be a daily visible sign of progress towards this spiritual ideal to create the appropriate spiritual atmosphere for God to be able to visit us regularly with His mighty revivals. Some relevant Bible passages to help and encourage us daily on the road to holiness and practical perfection can be read as follows:

<u>1 John 2:6</u>
Whoever claims to live in him must live as Jesus did. (NIV)

Those who say they live in God should live their lives as Jesus did. (NLT)

If we say we are his, we must follow the example of Christ. (CEV)

<u>2 Corinthians 3:5</u>
Not that we are sufficient of ourselves to think of anything as being from ourselves, but our sufficiency is from God. (NKJV)

It is not that we think we are qualified to do anything on our own. Our qualification comes from God. (NLT)

We don't have the right to claim that we have done anything on our own. God gives us what it takes to do all we do. (CEV)

<u>Philippians 2:13</u>
For it is God who works in you to will and to act in order to fulfill his good purpose. (NIV)

For God is working in you, giving you the desire and the power to do what pleases him. (NLT)

*God is working in you to make you willing and able
to obey him.* (CEV)

Before we conclude this discussion, it must be borne in mind that failure to walk in the steps of Christ towards the attainment of this spiritual ideal of perfection mentioned in Matthew 5:48 can provide the occasion for the devil and his demons to set traps for us on the Christian journey and cause us to backslide totally to lose our salvation.

So what do we do about this issue of holiness and desire for Christ's perfection as Christians? There is only one choice left to us. We must do our best to live and walk in righteousness with the perfection of God Himself as our ideal and divine standard in the power and enabling strength of the blessed Holy Spirit. To help us do this in practical terms, let us go through a list of some of the practical everyday sins which the devil and His demons can use to set traps for our feet because to be forewarned is to be forearmed. The list includes the following:

1. The sin of prayerlessness.

1 Samuel 12:23
*Moreover, as for me, far be it from me that I should
sin against the Lord in ceasing to pray for you; but
I will teach you the good and the right way.* NKJV

1 Peter 4:7

But the end of all things is at hand; therefore be serious and watchful in your prayers. NKJV

2. The sin of extreme worldliness and worldly cares.

1 John 2:15

Do not love the world or the things in the world. If anyone loves the world, the love of the Father is not in him. NKJV

Matthew 13:22

Now he who received seed among the thorns is he who hears the word, and the cares of this world and the deceitfulness of riches choke the word, and he becomes unfruitful. NKJV

1 John 2:17

And the world is passing away, and the lust of it; but he who does the will of God abides forever. NKJV

3. The sin of sexual deviation, fornication and pre-marital sex.

2 Timothy 2:22

Flee also youthful lusts; but pursue righteousness, faith, love, peace with those who call on the Lord out of a pure heart. NKJV

1 Corinthians 6:18

Flee sexual immorality. Every sin that a man does is outside the body, but he who commits sexual immorality sins against his own body. NKJV

4. The sin of intra-marital sexual abstention.

1 Corinthians 7:5
Do not deprive one another except with consent for a time, that you may give yourselves to fasting and prayer; and come together again so that Satan does not tempt you because of your lack of self-control. NKJV

5. The sin of extra-marital sexual relationships like adultery.

Matthew 5:28
But I say to you that whoever looks at a woman to lust for her has already committed adultery with her in his heart. NKJV

Hebrews 13:4
Marriage is honorable among all, and the bed undefiled; but fornicators and adulterers God will judge. NKJV

6. The sin of stealing what does not belong to us through dishonesty.

Deuteronomy 5:19
You shall not steal. NKJV

<u>Ephesians 4:28</u>
Let him who stole steal no longer, but rather let him labor, working with his hands what is good, that he may have something to give him who has need. NKJV

7. The sin of petty corruption.

<u>Luke 19:8</u>
Then Zacchaeus stood and said to the Lord, "Look, Lord, I give half of my goods to the poor; and if I have taken anything from anyone by false accusation, I restore fourfold." NKJV

8. The sin of compromise – encouraging and supervising others in sin without necessarily personally getting involved.

<u>Ephesians 5:6, 7</u>
Let no one deceive you with empty words, for because of these things the wrath of God comes upon the sons of disobedience. Therefore do not be partakers with them. NKJV

9. Sins of the heart like hatred, grudge, anger; interpersonal relationships – bitterness, boycotts, quarrels etc.

<u>Matthew 15:18-19</u>
But those things which proceed out of the mouth come from the heart, and they defile a man. For out

of the heart proceed evil thoughts, murders, adulteries, fornications, thefts, false witness, blasphemies. NKJV

10. Sins of the ministry and Christian service – deception involving money, sins endangering moral integrity, doctrinal integrity and financial integrity.

2 Timothy 4:3-5
For the time will come when they will not endure sound doctrine, but according to their own desires, because they have itching ears, they will heap up for themselves teachers; and they will turn their ears away from the truth, and be turned aside to fables. But you be watchful in all things, endure afflictions, do the work of an evangelist, fulfill your ministry. NKJV

11. Parental sins like favouritism, neglect of spiritual disciplines in the home, lack of Christian orientation for kids, quarrels in the home, constant disagreements in ways to handle the children properly for Christ, irreconcilableness.

Proverbs 22:6
Train up a child in the way he should go, and when he is old he will not depart from it. NKJV

Ephesians 6:4

And you, fathers, do not provoke your children to wrath, but bring them up in the training and admonition of the Lord. NKJV

12. **Workplace sins – colluding to defraud, corruption, dubious underhand deals and dealings, sexual harassment of females and other people's spouses.**

   <u>Colossians 3:23-25</u>
   And whatever you do, do it heartily, as to the Lord and not to men, knowing that from the Lord you will receive the reward of the inheritance; for you serve the Lord Christ. But he who does wrong will be repaid for what he has done, and there is no partiality. NKJV

13. **Residential vanity and community sins – quarrels, tensions, busy body activities, involvement with unbelievers in non-Christian social activities like drinking bouts, the use of narcotics, hard drugs, involvement with spiritually questionable personalities.**

   <u>1 Timothy 4:12</u>
   Let no one despise your youth, but be an example to the believers in word, in conduct, in love, in spirit, in faith, in purity. NKJV

   <u>1 Thessalonians 4:11</u>

That you also aspire to lead a quiet life, to mind your own business, and to work with your own hands, as we commanded you. NKJV

14. Spiritual sins like involvement in witchcraft, divination, spiritism, idolatry, sorcery and necromancy.

1 Samuel 15:23a
For rebellion is as the sin of witchcraft, and stubbornness is as iniquity and idolatry. NKJV

1 Chronicles 10:13
So Saul died for his unfaithfulness which he had committed against the Lord, because he did not keep the word of the Lord, and also because he consulted a medium for guidance. NKJV

Leviticus 20:6
'And the person who turns to mediums and familiar spirits, to prostitute himself with them, I will set My face against that person and cut him off from his people. NKJV

The purpose of the provision of this list of sins is to show us some of the practical evils God wants us to avoid completely to remain spiritually pure, holy and righteous. This can indirectly help us to be able to maintain the spiritual revivals and renewals granted by the Holy Spirit. Consequently, this list of sins must not be seen as a journey into legalism because there are several similar lists of sins in the New Testament such as the one provided in Galatians 5:19-21 which reads as follows:

> *"Now the works of the flesh are evident, which are: adultery, fornication, uncleanness, lewdness, idolatry, sorcery, hatred, contentions, jealousies, outbursts of wrath, selfish ambitions, dissensions, heresies, envy, murders, drunkenness, revelries, and the like; of which I tell you beforehand, just as I also told you in time past, that those who practice such things will not inherit the kingdom of God."* NKJV

Even the Lord Jesus Christ Himself provided the church with a list of sins in Matthew 15:11, 18, 19 which also reads as follows:

> <u>Matthew 15:11, 18, 19</u>
> *Not what goes into the mouth defiles a man; but what comes out of the mouth, this defiles a man."* *But those things which proceed out of the mouth come from the heart, and they defile a man. For out of the heart proceed evil thoughts, murders, adulteries, fornications, thefts, false witness, blasphemies.* NKJV

This list plus all the others quoted here must only be viewed as an attempt to provide all sincere Christians with a useful spiritual guide to assist them on the path of holiness and purity which alone can help them to run and finish the Christian race successfully. Secondly, it is meant to give us a clear picture of which sinful attitudes and tendencies must be avoided to prevent them from destroying our good relationship with God and drawing us back into backsliding.

> <u>1 Thessalonians 5:22</u>
> *Abstain from every form of evil.* (NKJV)
>
> *Reject every kind of evil.* (NIV)
>
> *Stay away from every kind of evil.* (NLT)

Bible Study and Personal Review Questions
1. Why is it absolutely impossible to receive God's revivals without first repenting of all known sins?
2. What is the unchangeable nature of God which always dictates this?
3. What is the importance of Matthew 5:48 to our being able to receive God's continuous revivals?
4. Is the attainment of the absolute perfection of God possible for us as Christians living in the sinful world with numerous sinners all around us?
5. Whether the attainment of this high level of perfection is practically possible or not, what encouragements can we receive from some of the quoted verses to help us to strive towards this every day?

6. If we always press on towards this perfection, what are some of the spiritual advantages this can bring to us on God's revivals and on our remaining in the Christian race?

7. What advise does the Bible give us on holiness and perfection in 1 Thessalonians 5:22? Is this not comparable to Matthew 5:48? What help can obedience to this verse bring to us daily as Christians?

8. How many groups of sins are presented in the list of sins at the end of this chapter?

9. What examples of similar lists of sins do we have in the Bible?

10. What practical help can a perusal and close study of this list of sins offer us in our desire for perfection and total abstention from evil?

CHAPTER FOUR
PRAYER AND GOD'S REVIVALS (PART 1)

<u>INTRODUCTION</u>

One cardinal feature of all revivals whenever and wherever they occur is prayer. This has always been the trend throughout the history of the church to the present day. The secret behind this is that prayer is the powerhouse of the church as well as the moving force behind all its vital activities such as revivals, healings, evangelism and successful engagement in the spiritual warfare. In the same way, the beginning, sustenance and tempo of all the revivals in the church and even at the personal revival level are always dictated by the intensity of the prayers of the saints. Consequently, we want to examine some special prayer programmes and other related activities which are invaluable to all the spiritual revival and spiritual renewal programmes of the local church. Let us do this vital examination as follows:

Bible Study and Personal Review Questions

1. Is it true to say that prayer has always been a cardinal feature in all God-given revivals?

2. In relation to revivals and all the other major programmes of the church, is it true to claim that prayer is the powerhouse of the church as well as the moving force behind all its activities?

3. How should the church of Christ regard prayer if we are serious to obtain God's regular revivals?

MOBILIZING PRAYER GENERALLY FOR GOD'S REVIVALS IN THE LOCAL CHURCH

By way of emphasis, we once again want to state that throughout the Scriptures and throughout the history of the church, there is no revival which has occurred anywhere without recourse to intensive prevailing prayer on the part of God's children. This is what the passage quoted from 2 Chronicles 7:14 highlights with the phrase *"...And pray to seek my face... then I will hear from heaven, and will forgive their sin and heal their land."* NKJV. In the light of this, we want to begin this whole discussion on revivals and prayer by examining the following Scriptures to help us to know which prayers to offer precisely to be able to move God's mighty and powerful hand to pour down His revivals upon us. The references are as follows:

SOME IMPORTANT REFERENCES ON PRAYER FOR REVIVALS

Jeremiah 33:3

Call to Me, and I will answer you, and show you great and mighty things, which you do not know. NKJV

Psalm 85:5-7

Will You be angry with us forever? Will You prolong Your anger to all generations? Will You not revive us again, that Your people may rejoice in You? Show us Your mercy, Lord, and grant us Your salvation. NKJV

Psalm 80:19

Restore us, O Lord God of hosts; cause Your face to shine, and we shall be saved! NKJV

Isaiah 38:16

O Lord, by these things men live; and in all these things is the life of my spirit; So You will restore me and make me live. NKJV

Jeremiah 17:14

Heal me, O Lord, and I shall be healed; save me, and I shall be saved, for You are my praise. NKJV

Psalm 51:10

Create in me a clean heart, O God, and renew a steadfast spirit within me. NKJV

If there is no revival without repentance, this same truth can also be extended to prayer for us to state categorically that there can never be any sustained revivals without intensive prevailing prayer! Genuine repentance always begins the revival but immediately thereafter, every other thing pertaining to the revival is done and sustained by intensive prayer. Immediately after the repentance, it is through prayer that the confession of sin is made to God for forgiveness and cleansing. Immediately after this, it is still through prayer that our supplications get to God including the prayer for revival, renewal and restoration.

So we always see from the Scriptures that whenever and wherever God's revival and rekindling occurs, prayer is incessant and prayer activities become rampant. It is through this prayer that the Holy Spirit imparts gifts to fuel the revival. It is through this same prayer that all the breakthroughs in the revival occur. It is still through this prayer that the manifestation of God's wonders and miracles occur. Still it is through this same prayer that all the people both within and outside the church see the mighty and lifted hand of the omnipotent God and either rededicates or give themselves to God.

The various references on prayer quoted above are meant to emphasize and amplify this truth. The first reference quoted from Psalm 85:5-7 amplifies this. It offers us the teaching that after our genuine repentance, we should specifically pray to God and ask him to grant us the revival. We read this in the statement, *"**Will You not** *revive us again, that Your people may rejoice in You?"* This is a specific prayer for revival, renewal and restoration which appeals to God's promise in Jeremiah 33:3 which reads, *"Call to Me, and I will answer you."* It is only in our revived condition that God always shows us great and wonderful things.

The importance of continuous prevailing prayer in revival is further emphasized in the third reference which reads in part, *"Restore us, O Lord God of hosts; cause Your face to shine."* These are direct pleas for God's revival and restoration. So we can make this comparison that if repentance is the ignition key which starts the car, the engine is the prayer which keeps the car of revival running continuously with the heavy load to climb all the mountains, to negotiate all the curves, and continue to run until it reaches its final destination. Revival and prayer are therefore like inseparable twin brothers who are seen everywhere together!

The last three references from Isaiah 38:16, Jeremiah 17:14 and Psalm 51:10 also do emphasize the importance of prayer in our search for God's revival. They do emphasize that returning to God in genuine penitence is not enough to bring us a full revival from God. Though repentance is an unavoidable first step towards any search for divine revival, they do emphasize that after our repentance, specific prayers and request for renewal and restoration must be addressed to God. This is captured in statements like *"So You will restore me and make me live"* (Isaiah 38:16c); *"Save me, and I shall be saved"* NKJV. (Jeremiah 17:14b); *"Create in me a clean heart, O God, and renew a steadfast spirit within me"* NKJV. (Psalm 51:10).

Bible Study and Personal Review Questions

1. What emphasis does 2 Chronicles 7:14 place on prayer in relation to revivals?
2. How is Jeremiah 33:3 related to prayer for God's regular revivals in the Church of Christ?
3. What specific prayer request for revivals are mentioned in Psalm 85:5-7? How should they help us generally to pray for God's revivals regularly in the church?
4. What specific prayer for revival is also mentioned in Psalm 80:19? How should they encourage us generally to pray for God's revivals?
5. What prayers for restoration and revival are contained in Isaiah 38:16? What lessons can we learn on general prayers for God's revivals at the general church level?
6. In which practical ways is Jeremiah 17:14 related to the prayer for revivals in the local church? Can't this be done regularly at the general church level?
7. In what ways can we say that Psalm 51:10 is a prayer for God's personal revival? Can we pray this same prayer for God's revivals at the general church level?

8. What is the value of intensive continuous prayer to the sustenance of God's revivals in the church?

9. Can any revivals begin and remain without continuous prayer by the whole church? If no, then what must we all come together to do regularly as a church?

10. What are some of the normal general church prayer programmes during which we can pray generally for God's revivals in the church?

ADDITIONAL HIGHLIGHTS OF THE GENERAL PRAYER WHICH BEGINS AND SUSTAINS REVIVALS

Revival is so important to God in the life of the Church that it should not be ignored in the normal programme of any local church which truly belongs to the Lord Jesus Christ. In the light of this, we want to propose the programme below as the vehicle to help us to seek and receive God's constant revival in the local church. The details are as follows:

1) Generally in the Church, we must always humble ourselves under the mighty hand of God to prevent any acts of spiritual rebellion and waywardness.

   2 Chronicles 7:14
   "If My people who are called by My name will humble themselves..." NKJV

2) At the family level, we should plan and adopt personal prayer schedules for revival daily.

<u>Acts 10:24b</u>

Now Cornelius was waiting for them, and had called together his relatives and close friends. NKJV

3) We should personally and corporately pray for God's constant revival in the Church.

<u>Habakkuk 3:2</u>

O Lord, I have heard Your speech and was afraid; O Lord, revive Your work in the midst of the years! In the midst of the years make it known; in wrath remember mercy. NKJV

<u>Acts 2:42-47</u>

And they continued steadfastly in the apostles' doctrine and fellowship, in the breaking of bread, and in prayers. Then fear came upon every soul, and many wonders and signs were done through the apostles. Now all who believed were together, and had all things in common, and sold their possessions and goods, and divided them among all, as anyone had need. So continuing daily with one accord in the temple, and breaking bread from house to house, they ate their food with gladness and simplicity of heart, praising God and having favor with all the people. And the Lord added to the church daily those who were being saved. NKJV

4) We must be serious to cry to God regularly for His revival through specially organized renewal and prayer events.

   <u>Ezra 3:11</u>
   And they sang responsively, praising and giving thanks to the Lord: "For He is good, for His mercy endures forever toward Israel." Then all the people shouted with a great shout, when they praised the Lord, because the foundation of the house of the Lord was laid. NKJV

5) Finally, at the personal level, every believer must constantly seek God's personal revival through personal prayer.

   <u>Psalm 138:7</u>
   Though I walk in the midst of trouble, You will revive me; You will stretch out Your hand against the wrath of my enemies, and Your right hand will save me. NKJV

Bible Study and Personal Review Questions
1. What are the key components of the proposed general revival prayer programme in this section?
2. How can it be followed and sustained both at the personal and general church levels?

HOW TO INITIATE AND ORGANIZE REVIVAL PRAYER CHAINS TO HELP BRING DOWN GOD'S CONTINUOUS REVIVALS IN THE LOCAL CHURCH

In addition to all the general revival prayer activities suggested above for general church application in this chapter to help us to pray to bring down God's revivals in our local churches, there is still the need to introduce another important revival prayer programme to complement those already mentioned and discussed. This is called the *Revival Prayer Chain.*

Remember that because prayer is our greatest source of energy, spiritual power and spiritual strength both as individuals and as a church, there is no known time when we can say that we do not need it in the church and in its numerous spiritual activities. Though we all know its importance generally and to the beginning and sustenance of God's revivals, one thing which often fights against its practical organization and implementation is the lack of a well-defined and sustainable plan which we can follow to be able to execute this prayer agenda all the time.

It is in response to this that we want to offer this simple revival prayer chain concept for continuous spiritual revivals and renewals in the church. Doing this is very biblical because the Bible tells us to have some well-defined plans and strategies for anything we want to do before committing them to God for His full spiritual backing to make them established. This truth can be referred from the two passages quoted from the Holy Bible as follows:

Proverbs 16:3

Commit your works to the Lord, and your thoughts will be established. NKJV

Commit your actions to the LORD, and your plans will succeed. NLT

Proverbs 3:6

In all your ways acknowledge Him, and He shall direct your paths. NKJV

Seek his will in all you do, and he will show you which path to take. NLT

The emphasis of these two passages quoted above is on the fact that it is always important to have some well-defined plans and strategies on any actions you want to undertake before committing them to God for His blessings, spiritual power and spiritual backing. Let us now begin our discussion of the revival prayer chain concept with the following important details:

Bible Study and Personal Review Questions

1. 1. Why do we still need another prayer concept like the revival prayer chains after generally knowing and discussing the importance of prayer to revivals?

2. What do the two references quoted in the introduction tell us about the importance of having specific plans and strategies for any actions we want to undertake?
3. How can we bring God into such plans to ensure their success after identifying them?

WHAT IS A REVIVAL PRAYER CHAIN?

It is a prayer programme of continuous prayer action. It can also be said to be a coordinated prayer programme which involves everybody in the church in the prayer for revival on a continuous basis. This coordinated and all-embracing prayer action always helps to bring down God's revivals quickly in the church and further helps us to sustain and maintain these revivals for them to remain permanently in the church.

Bible Study and Personal Review Questions
1. What is a revival prayer chain?
2. What help can it offer us for us to be able to receive God's revivals regularly?
3. Why is this prayer for revival called a "chain?"

MEMBERSIIIP OF THE REVIVAL PRAYER CHAINS

To make this prayer a true continuous chain in the church involving and linking up everybody in it, it must be organized to involve the following well-defined and well-organized groups in the church who can always come together every day or at least link up irrespective of where they are staying and located to raise their voices to God in prayer for His promised revival. Some of these defined groups of people can be identified in the church as follows:

1. Day of birth Prayer Chain (DOBPC)
2. Community Prayer Chain (CPC)
3. Family Prayer Chain (FPC)
4. Central Church Prayer Chain (CCPC)

Bible Study and Personal Review Question
1. What are the four groups which can be put together in the local church to compose the revival prayer chain?

DAY OF BIRTH PRAYER CHAIN (DOBPC)

A day of birth prayer chain seeks to group people who were born on the same day together to pray for God's continuous revivals. There are seven days in a week and everyone in the world is born on one of these seven days. So we can put together all those born on Monday both males and females to pray. We can do the same for all Tuesday borns and for all the other seven days of the week up to the first day of the week which is Sunday. This will capture every member of the church and involve him or her in the continuous prayer for revival. It is a prayer chain because when we start with the first chain of Sunday borns, the chain continues without breaking throughout the remaining six days of the week until it comes back to link with the chain on Sunday.

Though the revival prayers on the day of birth can be offered individually any time of the day from morning to night, the best method is for the church to agree on some specific times during the day in the morning, afternoon, evening and night during which the revival prayers can be offered to God without fail. If someone is unable to pray during these times because of some emergencies, he can then be allowed to pray during his own specially scheduled times before the end of the day.

Bible Study and Personal Review Questions
1. What is a Day of Birth Prayer Chain?
2. How can the Day of Birth prayer chains be organized in the local church to make them effective?
3. Is there anybody in the church who can be exempted from the Day of Birth Prayer Chains?
4. What is the best way to ensure that because everybody in the church is involved in the Day of Birth Prayer Chain all such persons will get the chance and the time during the week to pray for God's revival without fail?

COMMUNITY PRAYER CHAIN (CPC)
Community prayer chain is the putting together of all the members of the church living in specified but different

communities of the village, town or city where the church is located for the noble and important purpose of praying for God's continuous revivals. Though it may not be possible for all these people to group together in one location somewhere in the community before they pray, the prayer activity can still go on in their homes every day in the community wherever they are.

In some communities where a reasonable majority of the members live together in the same house or adjoining houses, they can come together and pray in one place if they so wish. But this should not become a rule but should be treated just as a case of personal and group preference. Starting community prayer chains is not difficult at all because nobody in the church hangs in the atmosphere but lives within a certain defined community in the city, town or village where the church is established.

While the Day of Birth prayer chain groups pray every day during the seven days making up the week, the community revival prayer chains will pray every day based upon the 30 or 31 calendar days of the month. The prayer coordinator will check and put all the established community prayer chain groups together and know their total number in the town or city where the church is situated. Then he will schedule some days of prayer for every one of these community prayer chain groups until all the 30 or 31 days of the month are covered.

Bible Study and Personal Review Questions
1. What is a community prayer chain?
2. What makes the organization of community prayer chains simple and straight forward?
3. Should community prayer chain members always come together in some specific locations in the community before they can pray? What is your personal position?
4. What is the best way to organize the community prayer chains to make them effective prayer channels in the local church?

FAMILY PRAYER CHAIN (FPC)
Every church is made up of families in the village, town or city where it was established. The only difference is that we have family sizes. While some can be described as small families made up of two people, some can be big families made up of five people or more. The important requirement here is that they must be members of the same family living together. In some communities, whenever the community prayer chains become well-organized, they do not repeat the family prayer chains because invariably, all community prayer chains are also organized around families in most cases. In other places this is ignored because they have a separate time for the

community prayer and another time for the family prayer. They argue that this is not burdensome because it only offers them more opportunities for prayer.

The family prayer chains are often organized like the community prayer chains. This means that when they are identified and created to pray for the church and its revivals, they are handled in the same way that the community prayer chains are handled. So some specified days of prayer are given to them on the church's one-month prayer calendar from the first to the 31st of the month.

Bible Study and Personal Review Questions
1. What is a family prayer chain? Where is it organized?
2. What is the difference between a family prayer chain and a community prayer chain?
3. What is the best way to organize the family prayer chains in the local church to make them effective?

THE CENTRAL CHURCH PRAYER CHAIN (CCPC)
The Central Church Prayer Chain (CCPC) is the prayer chain which is always organized at the central or general church level to bring together all the church members and involve all of them in the prayer for God's spiritual revivals on a continuous and permanent basis. Being able to organize it in the church successfully involves paying

attention to some important details including the following listed below:

1. It is a programme which is always organized to involve the local pastor, the local deacons council or the local body of elders as the situation may be in your church.

2. Because it involves a 24-hour prayer chain, the role of the individual members of the church is also needed to make it successful.

3. Before anybody is invited to be a part of this central church prayer chain, he or she must be made to understand that if we truly want God's revival, there is a price attached to this desire which must be paid. This price is the call to prayer. The Central Church Prayer Chain (CCPC) has been established to help the church pay this price for God's revival to come down.

4. It must be made clear to every person invited to be part of the CCPC that involvement in this prayer programme must be done with humility. Whatever we do in the church of Christ, the Bible exhorts us to do it with humility (Humble yourselves in the sight of the Lord, and He will lift you up – James 4:10) and with a servant's heart, and not as though we are more spiritual than all others in the church.

Bible Study and Personal Review Questions
1. What is the Central Church Prayer Chain?
2. How is it different from the other prayer chains already discussed?
3. Who are those who can be enlisted in the Central Church Prayer chains?
4. What are some of the important observations to note in connection with the Central Church Prayer Chain?

SOME PRACTICAL DETAILS IN THE ORGANIZATIN OF THE CCPC

1. It must always be conceived, planned and implemented as a 24-hour prayer chain. This will practically involve grouping all the church members who will offer themselves voluntarily into ninety 24-hour small prayer chain groups. Each small prayer chain group is thereafter assigned a specific time within the 24 hours making up a full day to pray for sixteen minutes within the 24 hours for God's continuous revival and rekindling in the Church. This will provide all participants and ultimately the entire church with the opportunity to pray for God's spiritual revivals and a harvest of new souls every day.

In situations where a church is too small to have enough members to form all the 90 small prayer chain groups, such a small church can form only 45 groups and commit the groups formed to pray for 32 minutes within the 24-hour period instead of praying for 16 minutes within the same period.

2. In addition to the central church prayer chain concept suggested above, a weekly prayer support team must also be instituted with the same aim of coming together to pray regularly for God's revivals in the local church. Its purpose is to join the pastor and the local leaders to pray before every general church meeting day of the week for God's power and special manifest presence to come down in the church before the full service begins. The same people must not be used every week. There must be variation to bring other church members on board to make everyone feel that he or she is also important and fully needed by Christ in the local church programme of seeking, promoting and sustaining God's spiritual revivals.

The duration of this prayer before the church service must be determined by the Pastor, elders and all the team members. The total number of people appointed to serve on this intercessory prayer group must always range between five and fifteen deepening upon the size of the church.

3. The local church must also organize a special permanent prayer band or "prayer tower" made up of different church members for every different church

service. During this service, they must be made to hide somewhere to offer continuous spiritual revival and renewal prayers to God from a point which will not disturb the general church service. Let it be emphasized that the same people must not be used at every general church meeting time since this will permanently deprive the participants of the opportunity of being in church to listen to God's Word for their continuous spiritual edification, personal growth and development. The number of prayer warriors selected for this prayer band can always range between five and fifteen persons depending upon the size of the church.

4. All genuine Holy Ghost revivals sometimes call for fasting. Fasting is sometimes necessary to give us impetus to pray more effectively and to get divine power to back our prayers. Consequently, to promote personal revivals, family revivals and corporate revivals involving the whole church, the central church prayer chain must occasionally organize fasting programmes involving the whole church.

One effective way to do this is to use the 9O small revival prayer chain groups already created to pray for the church every 16 minutes in the 24 hours of the day. Each of these groups will in addition to their 16-minute prayer every day also embark on a one-day fasting every 90 days. Because all the groups in the church are 90, if one group fasts and prays every day for the church, then there will be continuous prayer and fasting for the church throughout 90 days. So when the first group starts, and all the other 16-minute prayer chain groups follow it in a sequence, before the time comes for the 1st group which started the fasting to fast and pray again for the church, it will be over 3 months. This same 3-month duration will recur for all the other revival prayer chain groups also.

To help the entire church and the revival prayer chain groups to do this fasting effectively and consistently, the prayer coordinators must prepare a fasting schedule for all the 90 intercessory prayer groups to help them to know and to remind them when it is their turn to add fasting to their prayers. As a support initiative, a fasting and prayer guide has been provided in the appendix of this book to help all church members to get involved in this local fasting programme regularly and successfully.

Bible Study and Personal Review Questions
1. What first step should be taken to help us organize the community prayer chains very well?
2. What happens within the sixteen or thirty-two minutes of the 24-hour period of each day?

3. How does prayer take place in each of the 24-hour prayer chain groups before daybreak?

4. Can we then describe the central church prayer chain as a 24-hour prayer chain beginning and ending at 6am?

5. What are the advantages of the Central church prayer chains to the church at large and to the participants as individual members of the church?

6. In what ways can we say that a local prayer band forms an integral part of the revival prayer chain in the local church?

7. Who are to be the members of this permanent prayer band?

8. Where, how and when should they organize their prayer for local church revival?

9. What is fasting?

10. What is its role and important in the search for revival?

11. Whenever it takes place in relation to revivals how many people must be involved in it and why?

12. Is fasting not an outmoded practice which should be totally discarded in the church today?

13. What are your personal opinions and problems with biblical fasting?

14. What is the best way to organize this fasting for God's revivals using the revival prayer chain groups?

15. What must the prayer coordinators do to make this fasting and prayer programme regular and effective in the search for revival?

OFFICERS OF THE REVIVAL PRAYER CHAIN

1. Prayer Coordinator

   The prayer coordinator must always come from the local church leadership. His main role is to oversee the entire prayer chain programme to make it successful.

2. Subsidiary Prayer Coordinators

   Together with the pastor, the prayer coordinator shall appoint assistant prayer coordinators for all the prayer chains created to pray for revival in the church such as the Day of birth Prayer Chain (DOBPC), Community Prayer Chain (CPC), Family Prayer Chain (FPC) and the Central Church Prayer Chain (CCPC). The local pastor, the local prayer coordinator together with these assistant prayer coordinators will form the **prayer council of the local church**.

Bible Study and Personal Review Questions

1. Who are the required officers of the local revival prayer chain programme?
2. What role is assigned to each office?
3. What must each of these officers do to ensure their optimum performance?

4. When the appointed officers fail in their duties, how can this negatively affect the entire revival programme of the local church?

GENERAL OBSERVATIONS ON THE REVIVAL PRAYER CHAINS

1. This prayer activity must be seen as an all-hands-on deck matter involving everybody in the local church in the prayer for God's regular spiritual revivals and renewals.

2. When it is organized very well, it will bring constant personal revival to every faithful local church member because it will accord every church member the opportunity to pray incessantly for local church revival and thereby promote his/her own personal revival also.

3. Every church member who gets involved in this prayer programme whole-heartedly will get the opportunity to pray for revival once every day through the 24-hour prayer chain. Again, he will get the opportunity to pray for revival at least one day every week through the day of birth prayer chain. Furthermore, he will get the opportunity to pray at least one special revival prayer every month through the community revival prayer chain. These prayer activities will surely enliven and empower all faithful church members to be able to receive and maintain God's burning fire.

4. Thus, involvement in these prayer chains will surely bring great personal revivals and further encourage new entrants into the church to join and be faithful members of the local church prayer programme. This can directly or indirectly increase conversion and church attendance as a whole.

Bible Study and Personal Review Questions

1. Why do we say that the revival prayer chain concept is an all-hands-on deck matter? What does this mean and what does this involve in the practical sense?
2. What personal advantages can faithful involvement in the revival prayer chain programme bring to the individual church members? How can this help to speed up the revival we are seeking in the local church?
3. How can faithful involvement in the revival prayer chains help in the growth of the church and the integration of new converts into church life?

PROVIDING MATERIALS FOR THE REVIVAL PRAYER CHAINS

1. The local church must always make sure that revival prayer cards which contain the prayer topics of the local church revival programmes are always available for free distribution to all old church members and

new church members as they get enlisted into the revival prayer chain groups.

2. The prayer coordinators must be provided with whatever they will need to enable them function properly in sending messages to participants to remind them of prayer times and prompting them to their duties.

Bible Study and Personal Review Questions
1. What is a revival prayer card in the plan for revival?
2. How can they be regularly procured or provided?
3. What is its importance to the revival prayer programme of the local church?
4. What are some of the materials and equipment the prayer coordinators will need to make their work efficient and effective?
5. Generally, what must be the church's attitude towards the provision of all the materials needed to make the revival prayer programme successful?

ESSENTIAL REVIVAL PRAYER TOPICS FOR ALL THE IMPORTANT REVIVAL PRAYER PROGRAMMES IN THE LOCAL CHURCH

Continuous prayers involving many people like revival prayers without a prayer guide in the form of a list of prayer topics can sometimes lead to our missing our target. There is therefore the need to offer a suitable and relevant list of prayer topics which we can regularly present to the Lord before we conclude this chapter. This guide is needed so that we shall all say the same thing and carry the same prayer request before the throne of God all the time. We can always add to this prayer guide as new prayer topics on revivals come up.

Every good and positive thing in the Christian life is obtained from God by faith. This includes the prayer for God's spiritual revivals and renewals. Bible references on this are always clear and unequivocal. They include the following references:

<u>Mark 11:24</u>
Therefore I say to you, whatever things you ask when you pray, believe that you receive them, and you will have them. NKJV

<u>John 14:13, 14</u>
And whatever you ask in My name, that I will do, that the Father may be glorified in the Son. If you ask anything in My name, I will do it. NKJV

<u>Matthew 17:20</u>
So Jesus said to them, "Because of your unbelief; for assuredly, I say to you, if you have faith as a mustard seed, you will say to this mountain, 'Move

from here to there,' and it will move; and nothing will be impossible for you. NKJV

It should always be borne in mind that all genuine and acceptable revival prayers have two facets – "a praying against" and "a praying for" both of which must always be backed by faith. In response to this dual nature of all genuine revival prayers, the arrangement of all the prayer topics presented here has been done in two groupings. The "praying against" prayer topics have been put together as ten special topics in section one. The "praying for" prayer topics are also put together as ten special revival prayer topics in the second section. The details can be perused and used as follows:

PRAYING REGULARLY AGAINST SPIRITUAL COLDNESS AND SPIRITUAL DULLNESS

1. We should pray against carnality which is a major sign of spiritual coldness and spiritual dullness. This condition always manifests physically in the flesh taking over in everything we do.
2. We should pray against negative thinking – that is, always thinking negatively about the possibility of receiving God's spiritual revivals and spiritual renewals.
3. We should pray against the loss of our initial joy immediately after our salvation and new birth.

4. We should pray against the temptation to develop interest in the life of sin, evil and rebellion around us.

5. We should pray against any temptation and evil desire to stop working out our salvation with fear, trembling and great enthusiasm up to the end of our lives as faithful disciples of Christ. (Matthew 24:12, 13)
Matthew 24:12, 13
And because lawlessness will abound, the love of many will grow cold. But he who endures to the end shall be saved. NKJV

6. We should pray against any temptations to laziness and apathy towards personal Bible study, personal prayer and devotion and family devotion to prevent our losing touch with God and His strength daily.

7. We should pray for God to reveal and deal with any spiritual defects in any areas of our lives which can pull us back into worldliness, spiritual coldness and spiritual dullness.

8. We should pray against any forms of spiritual pride and spiritual arrogance which can lead to suppressed anger, inner and outward sinfulness and develop into any form of spiritual rebellion and spiritual retrogression.

9. We should pray generally against prayerlessness and against the "spiritual thieves" like spending more time than necessary with your television set, on the internet, on the social media and on sports and entertainment.

10. We should pray regularly for the strength to fast and pray for constant spiritual renewal and the infilling of the Holy Spirit in response to Acts 1:8 (*But you shall receive power when the Holy Spirit has come upon you; and you shall be witnesses to Me in Jerusalem, and in all Judea and Samaria, and to the end of the earth. NKJV.*) and Ephesians 5:18 (*And do not be drunk with wine, in which is dissipation; but be filled with the Spirit. NKJV*).

In addition to praying against some of the elements of spiritual coldness listed above, it is also important to pray positive revival prayers constantly. Maintaining revival is not a one-day act. It is a process which begins with your initial repentance and conversion but which must continue throughout your lifetime. This is the only way to receive God's spiritual power and spiritual enablement to be able to live in the world without being part of this evil world system. This is also the only sure way to be able to resist the forces of darkness constantly and to progress steadily in the Christian race as an overcomer until you reach the threshold of God's holy kingdom. ***So we need revival every day in the Christian life as we undertake the Christian journey.***

PRAYING REGULARLY AND DIRECTLY FOR GOD'S SPIRITUAL REVIVALS AND SPIRITUAL RENEWALS

1. We should pray directly for God's spiritual revivals, spiritual renewals and spiritual rekindling as Kind David did. (Psalm 51:10) (*Create in me a clean heart, O God, and renew a steadfast spirit within me. –* NKJV) (*Create in me a clean heart, O God. Renew a loyal spirit within me. –* NLT)

2. We should pray directly for God's spiritual renewal which will affect our devotion to Him, our commitment to Him and to His values, our commitment to a life of holiness and purity, our commitment to God's work in the church, and our commitment to evangelism and soul-winning. (1 Peter 1:15, 16) (1 Corinthians 15:58)

3. We should pray for God's restoration from all acts of backsliding, spiritual retrogression and spiritual backwardness to be on our feet again. (Lamentations 5:21) (*Turn us back to You, O Lord, and we will be restored; renew our days as of old. –* NKJV) (*Restore us, O LORD, and bring us back to you again! Give us back the joys we once had! –* NLT)

4. We should pray for God to renew our passion for heaven and firmness in His holy kingdom daily. (Colossians 3:1) (Matthew 16:26; Romans 12:11)

5. We should constantly pray for new infillings and fullness of the Holy Spirit to pave the way for Him to bring us constant revival, renewal and restoration in all areas of the Christian life. (Acts 1:8 with Acts 4:31)

6. We should constantly pray for God's full and powerful presence together with His manifest presence in the church and in our homes to empower us. (2 Chronicles 7:1, 2; 1 Kings 18:38)

7. We should pray for the full and practical manifestation of God's power in our personal lives and in the life of the church to bring about conversions, prayerfulness and victory in the spiritual warfare and in all spiritual encounters. (Matthew 16:18; Ephesians 6:12-17)

8. We should pray for the strong desire and boldness to share the gospel with our immediate family members, extended family members and friends and neighbours around us. (Acts 4:29; 28:31)

9. We should pray regularly for the revitalization of all the spiritual activities of the church which work together to bring us continuous spiritual edification – the pastors and spiritual workers, the prayer programmes of the church, the regular services of the church, the revival prayer programme of the church, the Bible study and Bible teaching programme of the church, and all other related topics. (Hebrews 10:24-25)

10. We should pray regularly for God's power, presence and support in the churches' spiritual revival and spiritual renewal programmes like fasting, revival prayer chains, mini revival services and mega revival services and all the rest. (1 Timothy 4:14,15) (*Do not neglect the gift that is in you, which was given to you by*

prophecy with the laying on of the hands of the eldership. Meditate on these things; give yourself entirely to them, that your progress may be evident to all. – NKJV) (1 Corinthians 16:8-19)

As we pray regularly for God's intervention to bring us immediate spiritual revivals and spiritual awakenings both at the personal level and generally in the church, such prayers must be based on Bible passages like Habakkuk 3:2 and Psalm 80:19 which can be quoted as follows:

<u>Habakkuk 3:2</u>
O Lord, I have heard Your speech and was afraid; O Lord, revive Your work in the midst of the years! In the midst of the years make it known; in wrath remember mercy. NKJV

<u>Psalm 80:19</u>
Restore us, O Lord God of hosts; cause Your face to shine, and we shall be saved! NKJV

CHAPTER FIVE
PRAYER AND GOD'S REVIVALS (PART 2)

INTRODUCTION

We have already mentioned and stressed the importance of prayer to all God-given revivals in the previous chapter so we do not need to repeat it here. What we are going to do in this chapter is to discuss how prayer activities related to revivals can be organized and sustained first as a source of regular fresh fire in the revivals of the local church and generally as a source of the great spiritual impetus we need to be able to maintain God's permanent manifest presence in the church and thereby maintain a great personal and corporate revivals granted to all His faithful children who are continually desirous of His spiritual revivals and spiritual renewals.

Specifically, we want to talk about mini and mega revival services and how they can be organized regularly and effectively to be able to bring down God's revivals in the local church and further help these revivals to remain permanently in the church of Christ without being lost through any negative negligence and apathy towards prayer. Whenever and wherever God's genuine revivals start through genuine repentance, they can only be maintained through holiness and continuous revival prayers which can be obtained through personal prayer, family prayer and general church prayer through mini and mega revivals. Let us start our discussion of mini revivals incorporating the following useful ideas and ideals:

HOW TO ORGANIZE MINI-REVIVAL SERVICES TO PROMOTE REVIVALS IN THE LOCAL CHURCH

1. WHAT IS A MINI-REVIVAL SERVICE?

    A mini-revival service is a special service organized in a local church with the express purpose of promoting God's spiritual revivals and spiritual renewals which can bring the believers back to a renewed commitment and devotion to the Lord Jesus Christ. In nature, mini-revival services are short-term, periodic spiritual renewal programmes which help genuinely committed believers to be able to keep God's ignited fire in them aglow all the time. So mini-revivals are always organized in between the major and mega revival services of the local church to keep the believers on their feet spiritually as far as God's spiritual revivals and spiritual renewals are concerned. In this, mini-revival services are comparable to pouring fuel or gas regularly into a great fire which has already been lit to keep it burning continually and intensely without quenching.

<u>1 Thessalonians 5:17</u>
Pray without ceasing. NKJV.

<u>Luke 18:1</u>
Then He spoke a parable to them, that men always ought to pray and not lose heart. NKJV.

Bible Study and Personal Review Questions
1. What is a mini-revival service?
2. To what can mini-revival services be compared?
3. What are the best times to organize mini-revival services in the local church?
4. What purposes are mini-revival services supposed to serve towards local church revivals?

2. WHEN AND HOW SHOULD MINI-REVIVAL SERVICES BE HELD?

Let it be emphasized that mini-revival services can be held as many times as a church and its local leadership see the need for them. The local situations in congregations differ from country to country and from church to church. Consequently, we do not want to make any hard and fast rules about the times and frequencies of mini revival services. However, it is worth mentioning that some churches in low populated areas devote all the evenings of the second or last week of the month from Monday to Friday to these services. In urban communities which are busier, three days in the week covering Wednesdays, Thursdays and Fridays are often devoted to these services in the evenings.

In bigger cities where heavy traffic during the week days makes these services difficult to be held in any of the evenings of the days of the week, these mini-revival services are held as weekend retreats covering several hours on the second or last Saturday of the month. Still other churches combine the last three days (Wednesday, Thursday and Friday) of the second or last week of the month with the weekend retreat on the Saturday of the second week or last week of the month. Whatever be the situation in your area, schedule the time when almost every member of the church can attend these mini-revival services in order not to defeat its purpose as a regular renewal programme for all.

Bible Study and Personal Review Questions
1. What is the best time to organize mini-revival services and how often?
2. What are some of the local factors which can influence the organization of mini-revivals?
3. Is it possible to make hard and fast rules on the times and frequencies of local mini-revival services?

4. What are some of the best times mini-revival services can be organized in the local church? What is the best time for this service in your local church?

3. HOW SHOULD PRAYER BE ORGANIZED EFFECTIVELY AT ALL MINI REVIVAL SERVICES? Prayer and the word of God together are the bedrock of all the genuine revival programmes in the church of Christ so we cannot discuss mini revival services without mentioning them. Therefore, let us answer the discussion question above by outlining some of the major prayer activities which form a major feature of all genuine mini-revival services as follows:

i. Generally, intense prayers should always be offered to God after every faithful preaching, discussion and exposition of God's word throughout all the meeting days of this service to enable the believers to pray to God for the needed spiritual strength to help them apply the truths expounded. We should never forget that the major purpose of the mini-revival service is to keep us constantly revived and fully renewed spiritually which can partly be done only through intense prayer.

ii. The Sunday service following the mini-revival service must always be treated as a special day of the revival service to give full meaning to the mini-revival service held during the week. It is therefore important to observe some of the following details during this special Sunday service:

Bible Study and Personal Review Questions

1. What is the importance of prayer and the word of God to all the revival prayer programmes of the church?
2. What is the importance of frequent prayers to any mini-revival services in the local church?
3. How effectively should prayer be organized throughout all the mini-revival services of the local church?
4. How should the Sunday morning service of the week of mini revivals be regarded in the local church?

THE SUNDAY MORNING SERVICE AFTER MINI REVIVALS

The Sunday morning service ending every mini-revival is normally declared as a special day of prayer in the church to crown the mini-revival service. On this day, those who for some genuine reasons could not participate in the general mini-revival service programme will be in church together with those who fully participated in them. So it is a day which must be treated as the climax of the mini-revival programme during which the following important activities must be organized instead of regarding it as the usual Sunday morning routine service. The details can include the following:

i.   Special prayer against spiritual coldness and spiritual backsliding.

ii. General prayer for spiritual revival and spiritual renewal.

iii. Bible Study or special messages and sermons on topics related to the power of God, the power of Christ, the power of the Holy Spirit and others related to revival and renewal should be treated.

iv. The prayer sessions can be organized using the list of 20 special revival prayer topics provided at the end of the previous chapter.

Bible Study and Personal Review Question

1. What are the four important activities which should characterize the Sunday morning service coming immediately after the mini-revival service?

Organizing the Special Post Mini-Revival Sunday Service Programme

i.   If it is a small church, the pastor can lead it for prayer to be offered on each of the prayer topics.

ii. If the church is a medium-sized church, the deacons and church leaders can be involved to assist the Pastor by dividing the men, women and youth into fairly large groups for the prayer.

iii. If it is a big church with several meeting places for prayer at the church premises, then the members can be divided and put into as many groups as the church has spacious meeting places for the prayer.

iv. In addition to the pastors and church leaders, other mature persons from among the members can be chosen to assist as leaders in this prayer activity.

v. To end the service well, prayer can be offered for the sick, for their healing and deliverance by the pastors and the church leaders.

Bible Study and Personal Review Question

1. In which important ways can the prayers for spiritual revival and spiritual renewal be organized during this special Sunday morning service?

4. HOW SHOULD THE WORD OF GOD BE HANDLED EFFECTIVELY AT ALL MINI REVIVAL SERVICES? This reminds us of the type of messages to be presented from God's word at all mini-revival services. The local pastor and some of the local church leaders can preach and teach on some of the suggested topics listed in this chapter. Alternatively, they can use the time for preaching to do group Bible studies and Bible discussions on the appropriate revival and renewal

related topics they want to treat. The Bible studies must contain interpretative and review questions which will lead the group members and the entire church to discover the truths which need to be emphasized.

More importantly, the pastor of the local church and the local church leaders can also lead the church to embark upon special biographical Bible studies (i.e. Bible studies based on some selected male and female Bible characters) and select the appropriate Bible characters whose lives portray virtues of revival, renewal, commitment to Christ and so on. Some of these characters can paint perfect character pictures for the entire church to follow on all aspects of God's revival. At the end of every Bible study, the pastor and the local church leaders can present a short summary of all the truths learned before the whole church stands upon these truths to turn into the period of intense prayer for revival, restoration and renewal. This is the sure way to induce true devotion to God and faithfulness to Christ.

Bible Study and Personal Review Question
1. What are some of the best ways to handle the word of God during the Sunday morning services after the mini-

revival programmes to help us avoid monotony and generate and sustain interest in the word of God?

5. WHAT ARE THE REASONS AND BENEFITS OF A TRUE MINI-REVIVAL SERVICE?

Though there are several major purposes for organizing regular mini-revival services, we want to discuss some of these reasons and benefits here to remind us that our regular and continuous involvement in mini-revival services are not a mere waste of time and energy but fulfils a very important spiritual purpose. Some of these reasons and benefits can be listed as follows:

Reasons for Mini-Revival Services

1. The first purpose is to pray to create the right spiritual atmosphere for God's full and manifest presence which is always responsible for all revivals to recur in the church so that all the members can renew their commitment to God without wavering.

2. The second purpose is to create the environment for new people in the church to be saved through the peaching and discussion of Bible messages pertaining to salvation and the New Birth.

3. The third purpose is to bring renewed spiritual strength to the already saved old church members

to help them to be able to run the Christian race and continue in the Christian journey.

4. The fourth purpose is to create the opportunity for people to seek and receive God's divine healing and spiritual deliverance so that as many people as are bound by the devil and his demons can be set free to be able to maintain the joy of their salvation.

Bible Study and Personal Review Questions
1. What is the first important reason for all mini-revival services?
2. What is the second important reason for all the mini-revival services of the local church?
3. What is the third major reason for organizing mini-revival services in the local church?
4. What is the fourth reason for all the mini-revival services of the local church?

Benefits of Mini-Revival Services

1. They offer us the opportunity to demonstrate obedience to God and to His commandments on prayer on a regular basis.
2. They bring into remembrance some of God's important spiritual and practical provisions for His people in His true church.
3. They give us the opportunity to demonstrate practical stewardship to God and to acknowledge

Him as the owner of all our resources both time and material.

4. They provide us with a new sense of God's presence by ushering us into a renewed environment of His holiness and power.

5. They offer a great opportunity for continuous spiritual renewal and restoration by creating the appropriate spiritual atmosphere for repentance and confession of personal and corporate sins.

6. They provide a big and invaluable opportunity continually to renew our fellowship and the covenant made with God through salvation which resulted in the New Birth.

Bible Study and Personal Review Questions

1. What are some of the important spiritual benefits regular mini-revivals can bring to the church and its members?

2. What are some of the useful personal benefits we can derive from the mini-revival services of the local church?

3. What are some of the practical benefits which can come to us from the mini-revival services of the local church?

LEADERSHIP OF MINI-REVIVAL SERVICES

Because of the fact that the local church can also think of organizing mega revival services which may involve the invitation of external speakers, evangelists and other men of God, it is advisable to leave the leadership of the mini-revival services to capable local leaders like the local pastor, the local evangelists and the local church leadership. The most important thing is to ensure that the Revival Prayer Chains are properly organized to be effective and fully beneficial to all the church members and the whole revival pogramme of the local church.

Bible Study and Personal Review Questions
1. Who are those to lead the mini-revival services of the local church?
2. What are some of the reasons behind our suggestion that they must always lead this important programme of the local church?
3. What are some of the best materials and resources available for the mini-revival services as suggested in this section?
4. Where and how can these materials be obtained for use in the local church?

IMPORTANT NOTE

Already prepared sermons and sermon outlines which can effectively be used as full sermons, Bible study outlines and biographical Bible study materials on all the topics suggested for mini revival services at the end of this discussion on mini-revival services are available for instant use from the following books written by the author and bearing the titles: A simple way to prepare and preach sermons from the Bible; Powerful sermon outlines (vol. 1); Powerful sermon outlines (vol. 2); Biographical sermon outlines (vol. 1); Biographical sermon outlines (vol. 2); Topical sermon outlines (vol. 1); Topical sermon outlines (vol. 2); and Special sermon outlines. All the books can be obtained from the following sources on the internet:

1. Go directly to google books and type "Stephen Adu-Boahen books" into the search bar.
2. Go directly to this internet link: www.amazon.com/author/stephenadu-boahen

SOME OF THE REVIVAL RELATED TOPICS WHICH CAN BE PREACHED ON OR DISCUSSED AT ALL MINI-REVIVAL SERVICES AND MEETINGS

It is your aim which always dictates your methods and practices. Your aim establishes the focus. Your methods and practices thereafter become the vehicle which lead you to your target. The list presented below highlights some of the important topics which can be treated at all mini revival services as well as mega revival services to help us realize our objectives. They include the following:

1. The nature of God (His holiness, righteousness, uprightness and purity)
2. The judgements of God
3. Creating and cultivating the powerful presence of God
4. Walking with God according to His will
5. Important principles of walking with God successfully
6. The importance of salvation
7. Understanding the three stages of Salvation (I am saved; I am being saved; I will be saved)
8. The value and importance of constant spiritual perseverance
9. Where and how to get power to maintain your salvation
10. The importance of holiness generally and to our salvation in particular
11. Understanding the Christian life as a race
12. Understanding the Christian life as a journey
13. The wicked purposes and evil intentions of the devil and his demons in the spiritual warfare
14. Seeing the Devil as an enemy and not a friend
15. Satan's arena and modus operandi
16. How to survive in all situations as a Christian
17. The importance of walking in total obedience to God
18. The predicted mass apostasy in this end-time period and how to escape it

36. Securing your future as a Christian
37. Destructive sexual deviations and sexual sins common today
38. Being the person Christ wants in His Church

SPECIAL CONCLUDING REMARKS:

PRAYER FOR THE INFILLING AND THE SPECIAL POWER OF THE HOLY SPIRIT AT ALL MINI AND MEGA REVIVAL SERVICES

Special arrangements should be made, and ample time should always be provided for persistent prayer to be made to seek the infilling of the Holy Spirit and the impartation of the divine power which always accompanies this in the light of the Bible references quoted below at all mini and mega revival services.

> Acts 1:8
> *But you will receive power when the Holy Spirit has come upon you, and you will be my witnesses in Jerusalem and in all Judea and Samaria, and to the end of the earth.* ESV

> Luke 11:13
> *If you then, being evil, know how to give good gifts to your children, how much more will your heavenly Father give the Holy Spirit to those who ask Him!"* NJKV

Matthew 3:11

I indeed baptize you with water unto repentance, but He who is coming after me is mightier than I, whose sandals I am not worthy to carry. He will baptize you with the Holy Spirit and fire. NJKV

Luke 24:49 with Acts 1:4-5

Behold, I send the Promise of My Father upon you; but tarry in the city of Jerusalem until you are endued with power from on high." NKJV

On one occasion, while he was eating with them, he gave them this command: "Do not leave Jerusalem, but wait for the gift my Father promised, which you have heard me speak about. For John baptized with water, but in a few days you will be baptized with the Holy Spirit." NIV

Acts 19:1-8

While Apollos was at Corinth, Paul took the road through the interior and arrived at Ephesus. There he found some disciples and asked them, "Did you receive the Holy Spirit when you believed?" They answered, "No, we have not even heard that there is a Holy Spirit." So Paul asked, "Then what baptism did you receive?" "John's baptism," they replied. Paul said, "John's baptism was a baptism of repentance. He told the people to believe in the one coming after him, that is, in Jesus." On hearing this, they were baptized in the name of the Lord Jesus.

When Paul placed his hands on them, the Holy Spirit came on them, *and they spoke in tongues and prophesied. There were about twelve men in all.* NIV

Romans 8:11
But if the Spirit of Him who raised Jesus from the dead dwells in you, He who raised Christ from the dead will also give life to your mortal bodies through His Spirit who dwells in you. NKJV

The main reason for giving time to this prayer for the Holy Spirit is that the major purpose and focus of every revival is to bring spiritual renewal and a new sense of holiness as well as a renewed sense of God's holiness to enable Him to pour His full strength and power on us to help us to overcome sin, Satan and all his worldly allurements. So, if we do not make time to seek this power of the Holy Spirit repeatedly at all revival services, then the main aim of organizing these revivals is totally defeated.

In addition to praying for the fullness and the power of the Holy Spirit generally at all these revival services, specific prayer must also be addressed to God for Him to *RENEW THE FULL FIRE OF THE HOLY SPIRIT* in and upon us as individuals and as a church to help bring the following advantages of *GOD'S REVIVAL FIRE* to all His children individually and in the entire congregation:

- Fire is a symbol of **GOD'S SPECIAL POWERFUL PRESENCE** to all His True, Holy and Faithful Children

  Exodus 19:18
  Now Mount Sinai was completely in smoke, because the Lord descended upon it in fire. Its smoke ascended like the smoke of a furnace, and the whole mountain quaked greatly. NKJV

  Exodus 3:2
  And the Angel of the Lord appeared to him in a flame of fire from the midst of a bush. So he looked, and behold, the bush was burning with fire, but the bush was not consumed. NKJV

  Exodus 13:21
  And the Lord went before them by day in a pillar of cloud to lead the way, and by night in a pillar of fire to give them light, so as to go by day and night. NKJV

  Leviticus 9:24
  And fire came out from before the Lord and consumed the burnt offering and the fat on the altar. When all the people saw it, they shouted and fell on their faces. NKJV

<u>2 Chronicles 7:1</u>
When Solomon had finished praying, fire came down from heaven and consumed the burnt offering and the sacrifices; and the glory of the Lord filled the temple. NKJV

- Fire is a symbol of **GOD'S OMNIPOTENT POWER** to all His True and Faithful Children

<u>Psalm 97:3</u>
A fire goes before Him, and burns up His enemies round about. NKJV

<u>Psalm 50:3</u>
Our God shall come, and shall not keep silent; a fire shall devour before Him, and it shall be very tempestuous all around Him. NKJV

<u>Acts 2:3-4</u>
Then there appeared to them divided tongues, as of fire, and one sat upon each of them. And they were all filled with the Holy Spirit and began to speak with other tongues, as the Spirit gave them utterance. NKJV

<u>1 Kings 18:36-39</u>
And it came to pass, at the time of the offering of the evening sacrifice, that Elijah the prophet came near and said, "Lord God of Abraham, Isaac, and Israel,

let it be known this day that You are God in Israel and I am Your servant, and that I have done all these things at Your word. Hear me, O Lord, hear me, that this people may know that You are the Lord God, and that You have turned their hearts back to You again." Then the fire of the Lord fell and consumed the burnt sacrifice, and the wood and the stones and the dust, and it licked up the water that was in the trench. Now when all the people saw it, they fell on their faces; and they said, "The Lord, He is God! The Lord, He is God!" NKJV

- Fire is a symbol of God's **DIVINE JUDGEMENTS** upon our enemies to bring us total victory and freedom

Genesis 19:24

Then the Lord rained brimstone and fire on Sodom and Gomorrah, from the Lord out of the heavens. NKJV

2 Kings 1:10-12

So Elijah answered and said to the captain of fifty, "If I am a man of God, then let fire come down from heaven and consume you and your fifty men." And fire came down from heaven and consumed him and his fifty. Then he sent to him another captain of fifty with his fifty men. And he answered and said to him: "Man of God, thus has the king said, 'Come down quickly!' "So Elijah answered and said to them, "If

I am a man of God, let fire come down from heaven and consume you and your fifty men." And the fire of God came down from heaven and consumed him and his fifty. NKJV

- Fire is God's Method of **SPIRITUAL PURIFICATION AND CLEANSING OF ALL HIS TRUE AND REPENTANT CHILDREN**

Zechariah 13:9

"I will bring the one-third through the fire, will refine them as silver is refined, and test them as gold is tested. They will call on My name, and I will answer them. I will say, 'This is My people'; and each one will say, 'The Lord is my God.'" NKJV

Isaiah 6:5-7

So I said: "Woe is me, for I am undone! Because I am a man of unclean lips, and I dwell in the midst of a people of unclean lips; for my eyes have seen the King, the Lord of hosts." Then one of the seraphim flew to me, having in his hand a live coal which he had taken with the tongs from the altar. And he touched my mouth with it, and said: "Behold, this has touched your lips; your iniquity is taken away, and your sin purged." NKJV

HOW TO ORGANIZE MEGA REVIVAL SERVICES TO PROMOTE REVIVALS IN THE LOCAL CHURCH

One other important way of promoting revivals in the local church is through the organization of regular Mega Revival Services. So we want to talk about mega revival services before we conclude this chapter. We want to do this by trying to answer some important questions about Mega Revivals as follows:

1. **What is a mega revival service?**

    A mega revival service is a special service like a mini-revival service which is also organized to promote local church revivals on a grander scale than the monthly mini-revival services.

2. **What are the major aims of a mega revival service?**

    Mega revival services are normally organized with two major aims in mind. The first aim is to bring spiritual renewal and spiritual rededication to the members of the church to be able to receive the needed spiritual strength to continue in the Christian race as it is done in all revival services. The second aim is to create the opportunity for the local church to grow numerically through oikos evangelism.

3. **What are the best times to organize mega revival services?**

    There are no specific and rigid times when mega revival services must be organized. Because local situations and conditions differ from country to country, from city to city, from town to town and from village to village, no strictly fixed times can be set for these services. What we can say for sure is that the time interval between mega revivals in most cases is either six months or one year. This means that they are either organized every six months or once every year. Some churches which do not hold regular monthly mini-revival services normally organize these mega revival services twice in the year – one at the beginning of the year and one in the middle of the year.

On the contrary, churches which hold their normal monthly mini-revival services usually crown these monthly services with one mega revival service at the end of the year. Whatever be the case, the most important issue is to organize it to be effective and effectual to bring the desired results of spiritual revival, spiritual renewal, spiritual edification and the growth of the local church which will immensely benefit both the old and new church members. In short, the number of times these mega revival services should be held must be determined by the local church in response to the spiritual needs of the local congregation.

4. **What is the best way to organize mega revival services?**

Many methods have been used by different churches in different parts of the world in response to local conditions but with varying degrees of success in the organization of these mega revival services. However, in majority of the cases, it always comes to light that the best way to organize this special revival programme to be successful and effectual is to organize it as a big indoor programme which takes full cognisance of some of the effective principles of organizing such Mega indoor church programmes. Some of these effective principles can be put together, observed and applied as follows:

Bible Study and Personal Review Questions
1. How can a mega revival service be defined and explained?
2. What is the motive behind all revival services?
3. What are the best times to organize mega revival services in the local church?
4. What are some of the specific things which go into the organization of mega revival services?

EFFECTIVE PRINCIPLES FOR ORGANIZING MEGA REVIVALS AS BIG INDOOR PROGRAMMES

Before we discuss the details of these principles in this section, we want to emphasize that this discussion must be done with the understanding that mega revival services are just like any of the other big indoor spiritual renewal programmes of the church. So if we want to organize mega revival services with any anticipated success and attain our desired spiritual goals, then some of the important general principles for organizing such big indoor programmes must be observed. We want to discuss some of these important general principles and guidelines in this section as follows:

1. **We must realize the importance of God's revivals and desire them in our personal lives and in the church.**
   Before any revivals can take place in the local church or in the life of an individual Christian, we must realize the need for revival and desire it intensely. So, right from the beginning we should ask ourselves the question, "Do we sincerely desire this revival in our lives as individuals and in the church at large? When we look at the society in which we are and take notice of the sinfulness around us together with the heinous crimes and incessant acts of evil, these should generate the intense desire in us to seek God's personal revivals which will affect the whole church and bring transforming spiritual ripples into the evil society in which we also live.

   But today, the desire for regular spiritual revival leading to constant spiritual renewal is non existent in the church of Christ. So the social degradation continues everywhere unabated. Therefore the first principle which should govern the organization of mega revival services is the existence of genuine desire for God's revival in our hearts. When we start on this note, then we have set our feet on the path to victory and success.

To help us to intensely desire and pray for revival in programmes like the mega revival services which we are discussing, we want to mention a few of the advantages regular revivals can bring to us as listed below:

i. Revivals promote perfect unity among Church members and deal with problems like church divisions, barriers to united church fellowship and burying of old grudges.

ii. It will renew interest in missions and evangelism which will ultimately empower us to work towards the fulfilment of the Great Commission.

iii. Revival always brings us new life leading to social transformation which in turn will also generate good deeds such as abhorrence of unholy practice and devotion to God in purity of life.

iv. Revival will always bring us fullness of joy. The Bible speaks of joyfulness as a great asset of the Christian life in statements like *"Rejoice in the Lord always. Again I will say, rejoice!"* NKJV. (Philippians 4:4) It is God's revival which restores this joy to us.

2. **Revivals and revival programmes must always be given priority in the church.**

   Regular mini and mega revivals must be scheduled and given priority on the Church's annual calendar. With regards to mega revivals, specific times for these services must be scheduled for the necessary preparations to be made towards them. This in other words means that we must plan our revivals far ahead to give our church members time to place it on their personal calendar as a spiritual priority.

3. **Budgetary allocations must be made for revivals and special revival services like mega revivals.**

   Nothing works in this world without money. The reason is that we are in a physical and material world whose activities are always dictated and governed by economic and financial forces. So if we schedule revival programmes on the annual church calendar without making any specific budgetary allocations for them, this action will remain a mere paper work.

   Many churches do not have any monies budgeted for spiritual renewal programmes and as such do not plan any budget for specific revivals like mini-revivals and mega revivals. But if we expect God to move and work His wonders through revivals, then we should plan to spend some money in preparing, promoting and carrying out the revival effort.

4. **For any revivals to occur in the church, prayer is indispensable.**

   After planning and scheduling revivals on the annual church calendar, the next important activity which must be planned and implemented immediately is prayer. All mighty revivals are borne out of prayer! To make this possible, the pastor must begin by selecting a prayer leader who can help plan and mobilize continuous prayer towards all mini and mega revivals.

   Prayer is necessary for us to get God's power to back all the activities of the church including evangelism and revivals. We should always remember that it is only God who can send us revival. God always does this through intense prayer. It is therefore proper to call upon Him to do this for us in the church before any scheduled revival programmes are organized to provide Him with the channels and opportunities to do this for us. Organizing prayer regularly for God's revivals and other renewal programmes is an open admission of what Christ said in John 15:5 that, *"...for without Me you can do nothing."* NKJV

5. **All revivals and renewal programmes in the church must be properly organized to bring us success.**

   Organizing any programme properly means bringing division of labour into it and creating the appropriate teams and committees to handle specifically designed assignments which can all work towards the overall success of the programme. Creating revival teams for all mini and mega revival services is of utmost importance. To start the creation of the prayer teams, the identifiable teams necessary for the success of the revival must be clearly defined and trustworthy and hard-working leaders appointed for each of them. Pick team leaders who are reliable, prayerful, sincere, honest and spiritually minded. Some of the teams necessary for mini and mega revivals can include the following:

i. Prayer Team

A prayer team assists the pastor in mobilizing and organizing prayer for the mini and mega revival services. This prayer programme must start far in advance of the mini and mega revival services. Sometimes they start their work six months or one year before the actual revival programme comes on.

ii. Invitation/Attendance Team

The main task of this committee is to work to ensure that all the important personalities who need to attend this revival programme are identified and politely invited to do so. The second main work of this committee is to ensure that all the identifiable groups in the local church participate fully in the revival programme. Invitation/Attendance Team must also have a leader and several faithful church members who will do their best to encourage all the families within the church to participate fully in the revival programmes. Their work also involves community survey to identify, encourage and invite unchurched and unsaved persons to the revival programmes.

iii. Ushers, Greeters/Parking Team

One often neglected and mishandled activity at big church programmes is warmly meeting, welcoming and greeting new people who attend our services and big programmes. This anomaly can be corrected with the appointment of this team. Ushers who meet new people at parking lots and lead them to the church doors are important. These greeters make newcomers feel welcome to the church premises and to the church programmes. Because of the nature of their work, it is critical that the Ushers/Greeters Team consist of people who understand what it means to greet people. They must mainly focus on and turn their attention to visitors and guests rather than conversing with the old church members they already know.

iv. Publicity Team

Nobody attends a programme he does not know and has not heard of. The main work of the publicity team is to publicize the revival event using multiple publicity strategies and materials to make the mini and mega revival programmes popular and well-known to induce attendance from within the community.

v. Stewardship Team

The Stewardship Team will work with the pastor and other leaders to make sure the offerings are taken in a proper manner. The funds received must be cared for and counted appropriately. The stewardship team may work with the pastor or other leaders during the revival event.

vi. Counselling Team

The counselling team must not be underestimated in its importance to the revival programmes. The Pastor or leaders of the church must train counsellors to be prepared to reemphasize the word of God and help those who make decisions during the revival services. It is important that the pastor does not become tied up at the altar talking with one person several minutes during the invitation. So other counsellors must be trained to help the Pastor at this critical moment of the service. Other people may be contemplating decisions for the Lord, but will not come forward if the pastor is busy with other people so the additional counsellors can take on these people.

vii. Follow-up Team

The follow-up team is critical to the complete success of the revival effort. The follow-up team is responsible for making follow-up visits to all individuals who make a public commitment during the revival services. This is done to ensure that all those who make commitments receive counsel and assistance in following through with their commitments.

In summary, the follow-up team is very important. They are fully responsible for the follow-up after the mini and mega revival services. They can do this by getting the new converts registered in New Converts classes, and in the appropriate Sunday School classes. Whatever they need to do their work to be able to keep proper records of people who make decisions for the Lord must be provided to make their work easy and successful.

6. **When members who take part in a revival programme become revived, they will not rest till they evangelize the world for Christ.**

Some people point out that revivals are really for God's people. This is true. However, when a church is revived, that church will be evangelistic in outlook. There are several ways that a church can have a new evangelistic zeal with the congregation prior to and during the revival effort. During revival preparation, believers should become more conscious of the fact that lost people are all around them, and these believers should begin to experience conviction about witnessing to these people as well. For this reason, the pastor or designated staff person should train members in the task of sharing their faith and inviting their oikos to the mega revival service before the programme begins.

7. **Soul winning and follow-up activities in the Week after the Revival Programme should be maximized to give more impetus to the revival effort.**

   The Sunday after the revival is just as important as the Sunday before the revival begins. Most churches often have a let down on the Sunday after the revival because church attendance is very poor. This creates a negative and discouraging atmosphere which can fight against the results of the revival effort. It is often said that God saves the best for last, and we should claim this in all mega revival services.

   The Sunday service coming immediately after the mega revival service must be treated as a special service during which the following important activities must be observed:

i. The Choir and the musical groups must be organized to sing very well to make the service very lively.

ii. The pastor must preach a sermon that has a bearing on revival.

iii. Those people who have been visited by the follow-up team on Thursday, Friday and Saturday following the revival should be acknowledged and invited to come forward to make open public commitments to Christ. Thus, the Sunday after the revival must be seen as a day of celebration and conservation.

Bible Study and Personal Review Questions

1. What is the first principle to be observed towards the successful organization of mega revival services?

2. What is the second principle to pay attention to towards the organization of successful mega revivals?

3. What third principle needs to be followed to help us organize successful mega revivals?

4. What is the fourth important principle to follow in seeking to organize successful mega revivals?

5. What is the number five principle we need to note in organizing mega revivals? Why is it important? What is

the sixth principle which is also important to be observed in organizing mega revivals?

6. What is the seventh principle which is also inevitable if we want to organize mega revival services with success?

WHAT IS THE OIKOS SERVICE WHICH IS OFTEN ORGANIZED TOGETHER WITH MEGA REVIVAL SERVICES?

To help this programme of mega revivals to be effective and successful in bringing both personal and corporate revivals to the old church members and in bringing new souls into the church through oikos evangelism, we want to explain all the necessary details about who an oikos is and how they can be reached for Christ through these mega revival services by quoting portions of the author's book bearing the title, *"Bringing your Oikos to Christ"*. All the important details can be provided as follows using the question-and-answer method to answer the following pertinent questions about the Oikos:

1. **Who is an "Oikos" and where can they be found?**

   "Oikos is a Greek word which is often translated "household" in the New Testament. In English, "household" means the core family; that is father, mother and their dependent children. In Greek, however, oikos which is the equivalent of our English word household has a broader meaning and usage. It included the core family, neighbours, co-workers and friends. In the broader sense, its usage also involved everybody with whom people had close and regular contact. In recent times, it has developed a wide terminology which includes such modern names and slogans like your extended family, your fishing pool, your world, and sometimes simply by the Biblical word your **'Oikos'.** Explained further with more family and relational details, you can say that oikos embraces the immediate family (Husband, wife, children), the extended family (Grandparents, uncles, and so on), dependants and assistants like servants, house helpers and their families; close and distant friends like classmates, school mates, ordinary friends in the community; and business associates like fellow workers, customers and so on."

2. **How can Mega Revival Services be organized to reach these Oikos for Christ?**

   i.   It is by teaching all the church members to understand Oikos evangelism.

   ii. It is by making all the church members identify the specific oikos they want to invite to the mega revival services.

   iii. It is by making specific prayer for the oikos part of the general prayer before the mega revival service.

iv. It is by making it obligatory in the light of Matthew 28:18-20 for all the old church members participating in the mega revival service to attend the programme together with an invited oikos.

v. It is by ensuring that all the invited Oikos join some of the evangelistic Bible study groups designed for all the invited Oikos during the mega revival service.

Bible Study and Personal Review Questions
1. Who is an oikos?
2. Where can your oikos be found?
3. What is oikos evangelism?
4. What is the importance of oikos evangelism to mega revivals?
5. What are some of the practical steps to follow to be able to combine oikos evangelism and mega revivals successfully?

THE PROGRAMME CONTENT OF MEGA REVIVAL SERVICES

Because mega revival services are always organized with some specific purposes in mind, it is essential to make all the programmes and activities of these services always responsive to and fully relevant to these aims and objectives. In response to this, mega revival services are always organized around the following programmes:

EVANGELISTIC BIBLE STUDIES

Mega revival services, because they also aim at soul winning are always organized as major evangelistic events. Specifically, they can be organized by incorporating evangelistic Bible studies in the programme. Sometimes evangelistic preaching is done instead of evangelistic Bible studies. More frequently, some churches resort to the evangelistic Bible studies instead of evangelistic preaching. Whatever be your choice of method, the most important thing is to remember to make it partly evangelistic which can be done by sometimes organizing it as a special Bible study programme or preaching programme as suggested above.

Several evangelistic Bible study groups can be created to facilitate this arrangement. The Evangelistic Bible studies or preaching should primarily aim at leading the participants to accept the Lord Jesus as their saviour during the programme. To achieve this aim, they must deal with topics on salvation, the New Birth, repentance, meeting Christ as a saviour, the value and importance of the human soul, seeking God, the abcs of God's free salvation and topics like that.

INSPIRATIONAL BIBLE STUDIES

To help those who are already committed Christians to benefit fully from the mega revival services, inspirational Bible studies must be included in the Bible study programme just like in the evangelistic Bible studies discussed above. Inspirational preaching on specially selected inspirational topics can sometimes be done instead of the inspirational Bible studies. There can be separate Bible study groups where inspirational Bible studies can be organized for the old believers at the same time that the evangelistic Bible studies will be taking place for all the invited Oikos.

These inspirational Bible studies or preaching must always aim at encouraging the believers to run the Christian race and to undertake the Christian journey with perseverance. As such, they can include topics like, avoiding spiritual lukewarmness, ensuring your progress in the Christian life, running the Christian race successfully, seeing the Christian life as a journey, seeing the Christian life as a race, becoming an overcomer in Christ, the three phases of salvation (I am saved, I am being saved, I will be saved), the power of prayer, the power in the word of God, defeating Satan and his demons with the power of Christ, overcoming worldliness, the danger of backsliding, the major causes of backsliding, how to avoid backsliding totally, the reality of heaven, the reality of hell, beginning and ending with

Christ successfully and subjects in this vein which have the capacity to encourage, strengthen and keep the old believers in the faith.

Bible Study and Personal Review Questions
1. What is an evangelistic Bible study or preaching?
2. What are the major aims of this type of Bible study/preaching?
3. What is the best way to organize this Bible study or peaching at all mega revival services?
4. Can a mega revival service be described as successful if it does not incorporate this type of Bible study or preaching?
5. What is an inspirational Bible study or preaching? Who are those supposed to benefit from this type of Bible study/preaching at all mega revival services?
6. Can inspirational Bible study/preaching be ignored at mega revival services?
7. What is the best way to organize these inspirational Bible studies/preaching at all mega revival services?

PRAYING FOR HEALING AND DELIVERANCE AT ALL MEGA REVIVAL SERVICES

Prayer for healing and deliverance must always form an integral part of all mega revival services. Sometimes some people reject the gospel because they have been blinded by the devil. They first need to be set free by the power of

Christ before the light of the gospel can enter their minds and hearts. In other situations, some people have Satan-inspired and Satan-controlled sicknesses which can only be cured when Satan and his demons are driven out of such persons. Sometimes some people experience multiple afflictions because of their demonic backgrounds which led them to bondage. So they need mega revival prayers to gain their spiritual freedom.

These are some of the facts and secrets which make the prayer for healing and deliverance a must at all mega revival services. The leaders of these mega revival services must be conscious and fully aware of this so that when the time comes for this prayer for total spiritual emancipation, everybody will be encouraged to get fully involved in it. Bible passages like 1 John 3:8 and others can be of great help in this prayer for healing and deliverance.

<u>1 John 3:8</u>
He who sins is of the devil, for the devil has sinned from the beginning. For this purpose the Son of God was manifested, that He might destroy the works of the devil. NKJV

<u>Hebrews 2:14</u>
Inasmuch then as the children have partaken of flesh and blood, He Himself likewise shared in the same, that through death He might destroy him who had the power of death, that is, the devil. NKJV

<u>Romans 16:20</u>
And the God of peace will crush Satan under your feet shortly. The grace of our Lord Jesus Christ be with you. Amen. NKJV

Bible Study and Personal Review Questions
1. What is prayer for healing?
2. What examples of this type of prayer do we have in the Bible?
3. What is prayer for deliverance? How can it be explained to the ordinary Christian?
4. What is the biblical basis of the prayer for healing and deliverance?
5. What are some of the reasons which make the prayer for healing and deliverance necessary at all mega revival services?

PRAYING FOR SPIRITUAL REVIVAL AND SPIRITUAL RENEWAL AT ALL MEGA REVIVAL SERVICES

Apart from praying special prayers for healing and deliverance at all mega revival services, another important prayer programme which must be observed everyday throughout these services is the prayer for spiritual renewal which is sometimes called REVIVAL PRAYERS.

These prayers must be organized based upon the truth that God has promised us His sure revivals when we prepare the grounds for this continuously in prayer. These prayers must have two major dimensions. The first dimension is the prayer for personal spiritual renewal for all the participants in the mega revival service. Time must be given to this personal prayer so that all the participants can take advantage of it to pray for personal spiritual renewal and personal spiritual revival. The second dimension is the general prayer for God's mighty spiritual reawakening in the church as a whole. So before the end of every service some of the following promises of God concerning personal and group revivals must be claimed through persistent prayer.

SOME OF THE PERTINENT PROMISES OF GOD ON OUR REVIVAL

Acts 2:17

'And it shall come to pass in the last days, says God, that I will pour out of My Spirit on all flesh; Your sons and your daughters shall prophesy, Your young men shall see visions, Your old men shall dream dreams. NKJV

Isaiah 57:15

For thus says the High and Lofty One who inhabits eternity, whose name is Holy: "I dwell in the high and holy place, with him who has a contrite and

humble spirit, to revive the spirit of the humble, and to revive the heart of the contrite ones. NKJV

Psalm 80:18
Then we will not turn back from You; revive us, and we will call upon Your name. NKJV

Joel 2:25
"So I will restore to you the years that the swarming locust has eaten, the crawling locust, the consuming locust, and the chewing locust, my great army which I sent among you. NKJV

Zechariah 10:1
Ask the Lord for rain in the time of the latter rain. The Lord will make flashing clouds; He will give them showers of rain, grass in the field for everyone. NKJV

1 Peter 5:10
But may the God of all grace, who called us to His eternal glory by Christ Jesus, after you have suffered a while, perfect, establish, strengthen, and settle you. NKJV

Colossians 3:10
And have put on the new man who is renewed in knowledge according to the image of Him who created him. NKJV

Isaiah 43:19

Behold, I will do a new thing, now it shall spring forth; shall you not know it? I will even make a road in the wilderness and rivers in the desert. NKJV

Titus 3:5
Not by works of righteousness which we have done, but according to His mercy He saved us, through the washing of regeneration and renewing of the Holy Spirit. NKJV

Ezekiel 37:5
Thus says the Lord God to these bones: "Surely I will cause breath to enter into you, and you shall live. NKJV

John 7:38
He who believes in Me, as the Scripture has said, out of his heart will flow rivers of living water." NKJV

Hosea 6:2
After two days He will revive us; on the third day He will raise us up, that we may live in His sight. NKJV

2 Chronicles 7:14
If My people who are called by My name will humble themselves, and pray and seek My face, and turn from their wicked ways, then I will hear from heaven, and will forgive their sin and heal their land. NKJV

<u>Acts 3:19</u>

*Repent therefore and be converted, that your sins
may be blotted out, so that times of refreshing may
come from the presence of the Lord.* NKJV

<u>Lamentations 5:21</u>

*Turn us back to You, O Lord, and we will be
restored; renew our days as of old.* NKJV

SOME OF THE SPECIFIC PERSONAL REVIVAL PRAYERS WE CAN OFFER TO GOD AT ALL MEGA REVIVAL SERVICES

The following are prayer points for personal revival and
spiritual awakening that you can use to pray and bring
back the fire of the Spirit into your life, church and
community.

1. Pray for absolute surrender to God and total
   dedication and commitment to Christ.

   *Also I heard the voice of the Lord, saying: "Whom shall I
   send, and who will go for Us?" Then I said, "Here am I!
   Send me."* NKJV. (Isaiah 6:8,)

   *That I may know Him and the power of His resurrection,
   and the fellowship of His sufferings, being conformed to His
   death.* (Philippians 3:10, NKJV)

2. Pray for total submission to Christ in absolute
   servanthood.

   He must increase, but I must decrease. (John 3:30, NKJV)

3. Pray for God to create a permanent thirst and hunger for righteousness in you.
    Blessed are those who hunger and thirst for righteousness, for they shall be filled. (Matthew 5:6, NKJV)

4. Pray for deep and intimate fellowship with Christ all the time.
    God is faithful, by whom you were called into the fellowship of His Son, Jesus Christ our Lord. (1 Corinthians 1:9, NKJV)

5. Pray regularly for the Holy Spirit to increase your knowledge of God.
    That the God of our Lord Jesus Christ, the Father of glory, may give to you the spirit of wisdom and revelation in the knowledge of Him. (Ephesians 1:17, KJV)

6. Pray for personal spiritual strength from God daily.
    The Lord shall send the rod of Your strength out of Zion. Rule in the midst of Your enemies! (Psalm 110:2, KJV)

7. Pray constantly for the fullness and the baptism of the Holy Spirit.
    John answered, saying to all, "I indeed baptize you with water; but One mightier than I is coming, whose sandal strap I am not worthy to loose. He will baptize you with the Holy Spirit and fire. (Luke 3:16, KJV)

8. Pray for God's material and spiritual prosperity to be yours always.
    "Again proclaim, saying, 'Thus says the Lord of hosts: "My cities shall again spread out through prosperity; the Lord

will again comfort Zion, and will again choose Jerusalem."". (Zechariah 1:17, NKJV)

9. Pray spiritual revival and spiritual renewal prayers daily to be able to keep God's fire burning in you.
   Create in me a clean heart, O God, and renew a steadfast spirit within me. (Psalm 51:10, NKJV)

10. Pray to God for the spirit of firmness and constancy in all His ways to be able to maintain your personal revival all the time.
    O God, my heart is steadfast; I will sing and give praise, even with my glory. (Psalm 108:1, KJV)

SOME OF THE SPECIFIC GENERAL PRAYERS WHICH CAN BE OFFERED TO GOD AT ALL MEGA REVIVAL SERVICES

1. Pray for God to revive you and put a new breath of His Spirit in you.
   So I prophesied as He commanded me, and breath came into them, and they lived, and stood upon their feet, an exceedingly great army. (Ezekiel 37:10, NKJV)

2. Pray for a total return and a rededication to God.
   "And I will pour on the house of David and on the inhabitants of Jerusalem the Spirit of grace and supplication; then they will look on Me whom they pierced. Yes, they will mourn for Him as one

mourns for his only son, and grieve for Him as one grieves for a firstborn. (Zechariah 12:10, NKJV)

3. Pray that the Lord would purify His church into righteousness.

   He will sit as a refiner and a purifier of silver; He will purify the sons of Levi, and purge them as gold and silver, that they may offer to the Lord an offering in righteousness. (Malachi 3:3, NKJV)

4. Let us humble ourselves and pray for God's permanent and powerful blessing which brings His continuous spiritual revivals and renewals.

   For thus says the High and Lofty One who inhabits eternity, whose name is Holy: "I dwell in the high and holy place, with him who has a contrite and humble spirit, to revive the spirit of the humble, and to revive the heart of the contrite ones. (Isaiah 57:15, NKJV)

5. Pray for the church to be filled with the love of God and the fullness of Christ.

   May be able to comprehend with all the saints what is the width and length and depth and height – to know the love of Christ which passes knowledge; that you may be filled with all the fullness of God. (Ephesians 3:18-19, NKJV)

6. Let us pray for the local church leadership to be fit for use by God all the time.

And when He had removed him, He raised up for them David as king, to whom also He gave testimony and said, I have found David the son of Jesse, a man after My own heart, who will do all My will.' (Acts 13:22, NKJV)

Therefore give to Your servant an understanding heart to judge Your people, that I may discern between good and evil. For who is able to judge this great people of Yours?" (1 Kings 3:9, NKJV)

7. Pray for an absolute love for and total commitment to the word of God in the Church.

   And that from childhood you have known the Holy Scriptures, which are able to make you wise for salvation through faith which is in Christ Jesus. (2 Timothy 3:15, NKJV)

   The burden of the word of the Lord to Israel by Malachi. (Malachi 1:1, NKJV)

8. Let us pray for the spirit of obedience to fall upon all levels of leadership in the church as well as all the church members.

   But be doers of the word, and not hearers only, deceiving yourselves. (James 1:22, NKJV)

   According to all that I show you, that is, the pattern of the tabernacle and the pattern of all its furnishings, just so you shall make it. (Exodus 25:9, NKJV)

9. We should regularly pray for the fullness of the Holy Spirit and the baptism with the Holy Spirit to come upon all faithful Church members.

   John answered, saying to all, "I indeed baptize you with water; but One mightier than I is coming, whose sandal strap I am not worthy to loose. He will baptize you with the Holy Spirit and fire. (Luke 3:16, NKJV)

10. Pray for God's material and spiritual prosperity for all the members of the church as proof of God's revival, renewal and favour.

    *"Again proclaim, saying, 'Thus says the Lord of hosts: "My cities shall again spread out through prosperity; the Lord will again comfort Zion, and will again choose Jerusalem."". (Zechariah 1:17, NKJV)

11. Pray for full dedication to the work of God in preaching and evangelism for all the truly revived members of the Church.

    But truly I am full of power by the Spirit of the Lord, and of justice and might, to declare to Jacob his transgression and to Israel his sin. (Micah 3:8, NKJV)

12. Pray for all church members to become worthy vessels for Christ after the mega revival service.

Therefore if anyone cleanses himself from the latter, he will be a vessel for honor, sanctified and useful for the Master, prepared for every good work. (2 Timothy 2:21, NKJV)

13. Pray for God's manifest presence and glory to be in the church all the time.

And he said, "Please, show me Your glory." (Exodus 33:18, NKJV)

14. Pray for all church members to be firm, steadfast and resolute for God after the mega revival service.

Therefore, my dear brothers and sisters, stand firm. Let nothing move you. Always give yourselves fully to the work of the Lord, because you know that your labor in the Lord is not in vain. (1 Corinthians 15:58, NIV)

My heart, O God, is steadfast; I will sing and make music with all my soul. (Psalm 108:1, NIV)

Bible Study and Personal Review Questions

1. Why is it important to give time to the prayer for spiritual revival and renewal at all mega revival services? What benefits can this bring to both the old and new believers?

2. What are some of the useful promises on revival upon which we can stand to pray for spiritual revival and spiritual renewal at all mega revival services?

3. What are some of the specific personal revival prayers we can pray at all mega revival services?

4. What are some of the specific general church level revival prayers we can always address to God at all mega revival services?

SPECIAL CONCLUDING INFORMATION:

PRAYER FOR THE INFILLING AND THE SPECIAL POWER OF THE HOLY SPIRIT AT ALL MINI AND MEGA REVIVAL SERVICES

Special arrangements should be made, and ample time should always be provided for persistent prayer to be made to seek the infilling of the Holy Spirit and the impartation of the divine power which always accompanies this in the light of the bible references quoted below at all mini and mega revival services.

Acts 1:8
But you will receive power when the Holy Spirit has come upon you, and you will be my witnesses in Jerusalem and in all Judea and Samaria, and to the end of the earth. ESV

Luke 11:13
If you then, being evil, know how to give good gifts to your children, how much more will your heavenly Father give the Holy Spirit to those who ask Him!"
NJKV

<u>Matthew 3:11</u>

I indeed baptize you with water unto repentance, but He who is coming after me is mightier than I, whose sandals I am not worthy to carry. He will baptize you with the Holy Spirit and fire. NJKV

<u>Luke 24:49 with Acts 1:4-5</u>

Behold, I send the Promise of My Father upon you; but tarry in the city of Jerusalem until you are endued with power from on high." NKJV

On one occasion, while he was eating with them, he gave them this command: "Do not leave Jerusalem, but wait for the gift my Father promised, which you have heard me speak about. For John baptized with water, but in a few days you will be baptized with the Holy Spirit." NIV

<u>Acts 19:1-8</u>

While Apollos was at Corinth, Paul took the road through the interior and arrived at Ephesus. There he found some disciples and asked them, "Did you receive the Holy Spirit when you believed?" They answered, "No, we have not even heard that there is a Holy Spirit." So Paul asked, "Then what baptism did you receive?" "John's baptism," they replied. Paul said, "John's baptism was a baptism of repentance. He told the people to believe in the one coming after him, that is, in Jesus." On hearing this, they were baptized in the name of the Lord Jesus.

When Paul placed his hands on them, the Holy Spirit came on them, *and they spoke in tongues and prophesied. There were about twelve men in all.* NIV

Romans 8:11
But if the Spirit of Him who raised Jesus from the dead dwells in you, He who raised Christ from the dead will also give life to your mortal bodies through His Spirit who dwells in you. NKJV

The main reason for giving time to this prayer for the Holy Spirit is that the major purpose and focus of every revival is to bring spiritual renewal and a new sense of holiness as well as a renewed sense of God's holiness to enable Him to pour His full strength and power on us to help us to overcome sin, Satan and all his worldly allurements. So, if we do not make time to seek this power of the Holy Spirit repeatedly at all revival services, then the main aim of organizing these revivals is totally defeated.

In addition to praying for the fullness and the power of the Holy Spirit generally at all these revival services, specific prayer must also be addressed to God for Him to ***RENEW THE FULL FIRE OF THE HOLY SPIRIT*** in and upon us as individuals and as a church to help bring the following advantages of ***GOD'S REVIVAL FIRE*** to all His children individually and in the entire congregation:

- Fire is a symbol of **GOD'S SPECIAL POWERFUL PRESENCE** to all His True, Holy and Faithful Children

  Exodus 19:18
  Now Mount Sinai was completely in smoke, because the Lord descended upon it in fire. Its smoke ascended like the smoke of a furnace, and the whole mountain quaked greatly. NKJV

  Exodus 3:2
  And the Angel of the Lord appeared to him in a flame of fire from the midst of a bush. So he looked, and behold, the bush was burning with fire, but the bush was not consumed. NJKV

  Exodus 13:21
  And the Lord went before them by day in a pillar of cloud to lead the way, and by night in a pillar of fire to give them light, so as to go by day and night. NKJV

  Leviticus 9:24
  And fire came out from before the Lord and consumed the burnt offering and the fat on the altar. When all the people saw it, they shouted and fell on their faces. NJKV

<u>2 Chronicles 7:1</u>
When Solomon had finished praying, fire came down from heaven and consumed the burnt offering and the sacrifices; and the glory of the Lord filled the temple. NKJV

- Fire is a symbol of **GOD'S OMNIPOTENT POWER** to all His True and Faithful Children

<u>Psalm 97:3</u>
A fire goes before Him, and burns up His enemies round about. NJKV

<u>Psalm 50:3</u>
Our God shall come, and shall not keep silent; a fire shall devour before Him, and it shall be very tempestuous all around Him. NJKV

<u>Acts 2:3-4</u>
Then there appeared to them divided tongues, as of fire, and one sat upon each of them. And they were all filled with the Holy Spirit and began to speak with other tongues, as the Spirit gave them utterance. NJKV

<u>1 Kings 18:36-39</u>
And it came to pass, at the time of the offering of the evening sacrifice, that Elijah the prophet came near and said, "Lord God of Abraham, Isaac, and Israel,

let it be known this day that You are God in Israel and I am Your servant, and that I have done all these things at Your word. Hear me, O Lord, hear me, that this people may know that You are the Lord God, and that You have turned their hearts back to You again." Then the fire of the Lord fell and consumed the burnt sacrifice, and the wood and the stones and the dust, and it licked up the water that was in the trench. Now when all the people saw it, they fell on their faces; and they said, "The Lord, He is God! The Lord, He is God!" NKJV

- Fire is a symbol of God's **DIVINE JUDGEMENTS** upon our enemies to bring us total victory and freedom

Genesis 19:24

Then the Lord rained brimstone and fire on Sodom and Gomorrah, from the Lord out of the heavens. NJKV

2 Kings 1:10-12

So Elijah answered and said to the captain of fifty, "If I am a man of God, then let fire come down from heaven and consume you and your fifty men." And fire came down from heaven and consumed him and his fifty. Then he sent to him another captain of fifty with his fifty men. And he answered and said to him: "Man of God, thus has the king said, 'Come down quickly!' "So Elijah answered and said to them, "If

I am a man of God, let fire come down from heaven and consume you and your fifty men." And the fire of God came down from heaven and consumed him and his fifty. NKJV

- Fire is God's Method of **SPIRITUAL PURIFICATION AND CLEANSING OF ALL HIS TRUE AND REPENTANT CHILDREN**

Zechariah 13:9

"I will bring the one-third through the fire, will refine them as silver is refined, and test them as gold is tested. They will call on My name, and I will answer them. I will say, 'This is My people'; and each one will say, 'The Lord is my God.'" NJKV

Isaiah 6:5-7

So I said: "Woe is me, for I am undone! Because I am a man of unclean lips, and I dwell in the midst of a people of unclean lips; for my eyes have seen the King, the Lord of hosts." Then one of the seraphim flew to me, having in his hand a live coal which he had taken with the tongs from the altar. And he touched my mouth with it, and said: "Behold, this has touched your lips; your iniquity is taken away, and your sin purged." NKJV

www.ingramcontent.com/pod-product-compliance
Lightning Source LLC
Chambersburg PA
CBHW061443150726
47987CB00001B/319